A CASE OF FINE CHINA

A CASE OF FINE CHINA

The story of the founding of
Royal Crown Derby
1875-1890

by
Hugh Gibson

©Hugh Gibson 1993
First published in Great Britain 1993
by The Royal Crown Derby
Porcelain Company Limited, Osmaston Road
Derby DE3 8JZ

Typeset at Deanwood Studio Ltd

Printed and bound in Great Britain
by Wood Mitchell & Co. Ltd.

ISBN 0 9520764 0 3

Introduction

*I*n the mid 1870's a group of individuals formed a company in Derby to manufacture porcelain on a site on the Osmaston Road. The Company was called the "Derby Crown Porcelain Company," although later, in 1890 its name was changed by Royal Command to the "Royal Crown Derby Porcelain Company," which it remains to this day.

Derby had been famous for its Porcelain since the mid 18th century, when the Duesbury family established a manufactory which gained a reputation for the highest artistic and technical quality. By the end of the century it was unrivalled at the quality end of the market, except perhaps by foreign (invariably state-subsidised) competitors, but the first part of the nineteenth century saw a decline and in 1848 the manufactory closed. Despite the efforts of a small group of china workers from the old firm carrying on business at the King Street works, it seemed as though the great days of Derby Porcelain were numbered.

But it was not to be so. This new group of individuals put Derby Porcelain firmly back on the map, and more than a century later, Royal Crown Derby still thrives and enjoys a reputation second to none. The debt owed to these men by those who work in the present day Company, and indeed by their customers, is enormous.

Until 1992 very little was known about the story of the birth of the Company. There have been meticulous and fascinating studies of the wares and of the artists of Royal Crown Derby, primarily by John Twitchett F.R.S.A, the curator of the Company's museum. His book "Royal Crown Derby" is the Bible for the collector and student of late 19th and early 20th century Derby ceramics. But the extraordinary business story which lay behind the wares remained undiscovered and untold.

Gilbert Bradley, Chairman of the Derby Porcelain International Society, whose object is to promote the study of

Derby Porcelain, asked me to give a talk at the Society's weekend seminar at Oxford in January 1992. As Managing Director of the present day Company he wanted me to tell the story of the Company's birth from the business point of view. I agreed, not realising that as soon as I began to look beneath the covers of time, I would find myself drawn ineluctably into the discovery and gradual piecing together of a remarkable story.

It soon became clear that I had more material than could be covered in a single lecture, and I decided to write out the whole story in full, and then to edit it drastically for the purpose of the talk. I gave the lecture and some members of the audience were kind enough to suggest that it should be published in its fuller form. This monograph is the result.

Hugh Gibson
The Royal Crown Derby Porcelain Co. Ltd
Osmaston Road
Derby
October 1992

Contents

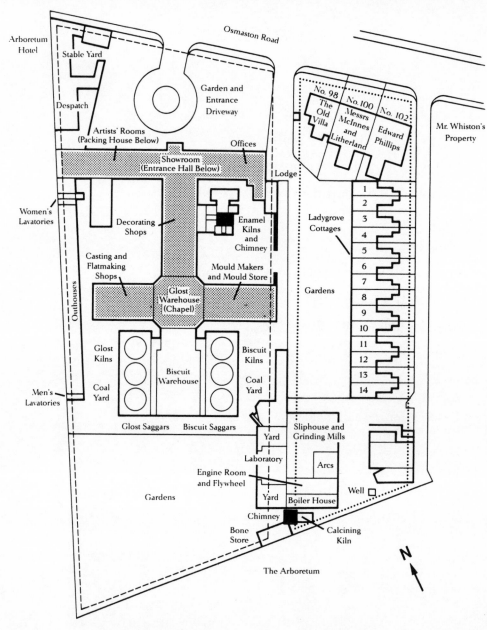

Arboretum Hotel

Osmaston Road

Stable Yard

Despatch

Garden and Entrance Driveway

No. 98 The Old Villa

No. 100 Messrs McInnes and Litherland

No. 102 Edward Phillips

Mr. Whiston's Property

Artists' Rooms (Packing House Below)

Offices

Showroom (Entrance Hall Below)

Lodge

Women's Lavatories

Decorating Shops

Enamel Kilns and Chimney

Ladygrove Cottages

1
2
3
4
5
6
7
8
9
10
11
12
13
14

Casting and Flatmaking Shops

Mould Makers and Mould Store

Gardens

Outhouses

Glost Warehouse (Chapel)

Glost Kilns

Biscuit Kilns

Biscuit Warehouse

Coal Yard

Coal Yard

Men's Lavatories

Glost Saggars

Biscuit Saggars

Yard

Sliphouse and Grinding Mills

Laboratory

Arcs

Engine Room and Flywheel

Yard

Well

Gardens

Boiler House

Chimney

Bone Store

Calcining Kiln

N

The Arboretum

.... Boundary of Ladygrove property, purchased by Litherland and Phillips in 1875

- - - - - Boundary of Board of Guardians' property, purchased 1876

▒▒▒▒▒ Extent of original workhouse building in 1876

1. Worcester Origins

*T*here must be very many easier ways of making money than in a fine china business. The trade is highly cyclical, highly skill and labour intensive, requires a great deal of capital equipment and working capital in stocks, the processes are legion, highly complex and volatile; money is made only when order books are full and all the parts are working in perfect harmony. To start up such a business from the beginning could be considered at the least, rash. Who would want to do such a thing, and why?

Pondering this question, I put it to a foreign friend of mine from the porcelain tableware industry, who was at that moment engaged in starting up a new business. His immediate answer was "Frustration." Working for years in a large china company, whose owners lacked interest in development and expansion, seeing all sorts of opportunities missed, finally he snapped, left his employers and collected a group of colleagues and backers to build a new business from the beginning to his own model. Was this the key, I wondered, to the foundation of Derby Crown Porcelain? We shall see, as the story unfolds.

Who, then, were the principal members of the cast of personalities involved in establishing this business, and what were their motives? How did they go about it? What were the obstacles which lay in their path, and how did they overcome them? Finally, to what extent were all their efforts rewarded with success?

The first and leading member of the cast, indeed the hero of the piece, was Edward Phillips, who was born in 1816 in Harley Street, London.

He came from a family who played an important role in china and glass retailing in London from the early 19th (or perhaps earlier) to the early 20th century. In the previous generation there were at least two brothers Jonathan and Jacob, and Jonathan kept a very well known china shop at 358 and 359

Oxford Street. Jacob spent some years in the 1820's as a manufacturer in Stoke, and is recorded as tenant of the Church works in Hanley. (1) It is not clear whether Edward was the son of either of these brothers, or of another unknown, but it is clear that he must have belonged to a cadet branch, because his two cousins, William and George, inherited the business and expanded it, opening another branch at 155 New Bond Street. (2) Edward's brother, another Jonathan, emigrated to Canada, (3) while Edward himself decided that even though there was no place for him in the family business, he would make his own way in the china and glass industry. He began his career representing Charles Meigh and Sons, of the Old Hall Pottery in Hanley, and also Thomas Webb, the famous Stourbridge manufacturers of crystal. He worked in this capacity for several years, becoming well known in the trade with a reputation as a persistent and effective salesman. (4)

After some time he changed the direction of his career by setting up as an enamel colour maker, and this in turn led him into manufacturing. He settled in Hanley running two businesses of his own, one decorating white china, (5) the other manufacturing crystal. These gave him a very good living but by the 1860's, in his mid 40's, he must have realised that to spend the rest of his life as a small-time business man in Hanley was insufficiently challenging.

It was in 1862 that a major challenge presented itself, and it is at this point that the second member of the cast enters the story; William Litherland.

William Litherland was a self-made retailer who according to legend began his retailing as an "itinerant with pots and pans and jugs." He was born in Leicestershire in 1803, and both he and his brother Thomas began their careers selling china from baskets in the squares of market towns. A family legend describes their sales technique of that time: "The two brothers Litherland would approach the square on a market day from opposite ends of the town, carrying baskets of ware on their backs, meet and start a quarrel about whose pitch was which; this drew a crowd, and when they judged it was big enough, the quarrel was settled and business could begin!" (6) By the 1860's he was evidently a pillar of the establishment both in Liverpool and in the world of china and glass. As well as his shop, he had business interests in the Adelphi Bank and in the Adelphi Hotel in Liverpool. This description of him appeared after his death in the Liverpool Daily Post:

WILLIAM LITHERLAND

"His shop and he were remarkable.....with the suavity and politic civility of an old fashioned salesman, he combined sturdiness of opinion and expression. His taste and knowledge of ceramic art......were self taught.......they were learnt in the daily market place of a business which early developed into one of exceptional importance.....he was cleverness itself in keeping up with the times......there were few such crockery shops in England. He knew no French but always went over to Paris to do his buying......he knew everybody who was anybody in Liverpool during the last half century." (7)

In 1862 there arose a remarkable opportunity and one could justifiably claim that this was the origin of the events leading to the founding of our Company. At the old Diglis China Works in Worcester the partnership of Kerr and Binns had floundered. The ten year partnership had been one of great technical and artistic innovation and there had been a good deal of building and renovation at the Works. Binns took credit for the artistic success; Kerr took the blame for the commercial failure, for the financial performance was miserable, and he returned whence he came to Ireland. Binns and the Worcester business needed new money to pay off the debt and invest in the factory, and they needed a good practical and commercial potter.

Litherland, one of Worcester's major customers, will have

RICHARD BINNS

been well aware of these developments. It seems highly likely that it was he who persuaded Phillips to move there and restore the company's fortunes. Against the advice of his friends, Phillips sold his businesses, and invested all the proceeds and indeed nearly everything he had in the newly formed Royal Worcester Company. He bought 20 of the 80 shares issued, and William Litherland himself bought a further four. Edward Phillips and Richard Binns became joint Managing Directors. (8)

The next thirteen years were summed up, in Phillips's obituary, as follows:

"It is not necessary to allude further to Worcester than to say that when Mr. Phillips went there it was almost as a forlorn hope, but by his unceasing energy – working from six in the morning, and then late in the evening at home, travelling and personally superintending the multifarious details – he left the Worcester concern free from difficulties. The Company has since paid, and is still paying, ten per cent to its shareholders." (9)

And yet, in 1875 Edward Phillips left Royal Worcester to set up a new china business from the beginning. Why on earth should he have wished to do such a thing? Here was a man who had invested everything he had both financially and in personal effort in Royal Worcester. He had achieved a remarkable success over a period of thirteen years. He was 59 years old. If the key to it was, as my friend suggested, frustration, then frustration over what?

Every forward-thinking production man has a desire for new buildings and new equipment. A pottery factory has a multiplicity of interlinked departments, and their juxtaposition vitally affects the flow of work-in-progress from one process to another, and therefore efficiency. The Diglis Works, in the early 19th century, had been somewhat of a jumble of buildings. They had of course been greatly expanded, as the business progressed, but they had to some extent, like Topsy, "just growed." The first Company Report in 1863 admitted that the factory was in a very poor state, and over £1,000 was needed to put it in order.

Phillips however wanted more than an improved, or even rebuilt factory. He had a passionate belief that a factory, particularly a china factory need not be a "dark satanic mill." The factory should be attractive, well ventilated and with proper sanitary arrangements, a pleasure to work in, or to visit, and should be surrounded by greenery and nature from which its artists could gain inspiration.

He and Binns nearly realised this dream in 1865, when the Company bought the Arboretum Gardens and drew up plans for a completely new factory, to be built on the adjacent land. The design bears an uncanny resemblance to the Derby Crown Porcelain Works, built 12 years later. Unfortunately this scheme fell through for lack of finance, and it must have been a great disappointment indeed, both to Binns and to Phillips.

Nevertheless, the business began to prosper, and money was spent on expanding and improving the existing works; in 1871 £1,500 was spent, in 1872, £3,000 of 6% debenture shares were raised for the same purpose. In 1874 "considerable extensions" were discussed at a special meeting of the Company, and it was agreed that more money was to be raised. All this may well have been moving too slowly for Phillips, and a source of frustration. But this alone, it seemed to me, was insufficient to cause Phillips to leave.

I therefore wrote to Harry Frost, Curator at Royal Worcester, and asked him to search in the Company's Minute Books for any further clues, or signs of stress which could have precipitated his departure: a row with Binns, perhaps. Mr. Frost replied with a dramatic discovery. Edward Phillips left because he was sacked. Sacked because either he or Binns had to go.

It is clear that relations between the two men had been strained, from at least the early '70's. Of the two men, Binns clearly held the limelight; Binns had the artistic ideas, Phillips had the more mundane task of turning them into reality. Furthermore, Binns appears to have had the ear of the non-executive Board members. Phillips's supporter, William Litherland unfortunately was not a Board member.

The minutes of the Company's Board, like all minutes, say no more than they have to, but one or two entries contain clues.

For example: Phillips has told some builders that while they were on site they might as well build the extra storey he wanted added to the mould chamber. This had not been sanctioned by the Board, and the minutes indicate the Board's displeasure.

In another entry, they discuss the problems of running the London showroom; it is stated that they need a man of Phillips's calibre to run the showroom. Would he consider going to London permanently to do this? Phillips of course refuses this extraordinary proposal.

In August 1874 the Board consider the tremendous success of the Company at the London and Vienna exhibitions, and recommend that Mr. Binns be awarded 300 guineas as a special bonus. Nothing for Mr. Phillips, who no doubt was concerning himself with the enormous cost of these exercises, and the problem of where to store all the unsold exhibition pieces still visible in Harry Frost's Museum.

At the next and special meeting of the Board it is reported that a letter of support for Binns's bonus has been received from Mr. Fenton, but a letter from Mr. William Litherland disapproves.

It is also worth noting that whereas the salaries of the two Managing Directors had begun as equal, by 1874 Binns was earning £800 basic annual salary compared to Phillips's £600.

The final and fatal issue was the London Showroom. The Company needed more space, and the new landlords of their Charterhouse Street premises were proposing to build extended accommodation for them. Phillips also had a proposal for new showrooms at a site opposite the Old Bailey. In December 1874 the Board declared itself unhappy with both proposals and instructed the Managing Directors to look for possible alternatives.

It appears that Phillips brought the Charterhouse Street proposal to the next Board meeting of February 1st 1875 as his recommendation. Binns reviewed the proposal and recommended that it should be turned down. The Chairman, Mr. Abell, rubbing salt into the wound, instructed the Secretary to write to the landlords to that effect. There then seems to have been an eruption. The two Managing Directors were subsequently asked to leave the room and the Board decided to enter the following in the minute book:

"The continued antagonism which exists between the Managing Directors and its evil effects on the conduct of the Company's business and the interests of the Shareholders received the anxious consideration of the Board.

"The Directors deeply regret that the efforts which they have made for years to arrange matters and bring about a better understanding between them have altogether failed and it now appears to them absolutely necessary to alter this state of things, and the Board after the fullest deliberation and after having heard the statements of both gentlemen unanimously came to the resolution that a meeting of the Company be called for the purpose of giving the notice to Mr. Phillips required by the twelfth article of association, unless Mr. Phillips shall in the meantime send in his resignation to the Board, and that Mr. Phillips have until the next meeting of the Board (now fixed for February 27th) to consider this resolution and intimate his decision to the Board.

"The foregoing resolution was read to Mr. Phillips by the Chairman and the Secretary was instructed to give Mr. Phillips a copy of it."

As is normal in such circumstances a settlement with Phillips was reached, in which he agreed to resign and in return would be paid his full salary of £600 for the following year (June 1875 to June 1876) on condition that he did not engage in the china business either as manufacturer or as dealer during that period.

Phillips's last request to Royal Worcester's Board in August 1875 was that it sanction a circular to the trade announcing his retirement from Royal Worcester, and declaring in the last paragraph that his contacts with his former customers would "not altogether cease as it is my intention ultimately to return to business." The Board refused to allow this last paragraph. (10)

Edward Phillips, together with his partner and backer William Litherland, in fact was laying new plans already by the summer of 1875. Plans motivated not simply by frustration, but by anger, humiliation, thwarted ambition and a desire to prove to himself and the world that he could realise his dreams without Mr. Binns and the Board of the Royal Worcester Porcelain Company.

2. Setting up in Derby

*E*dward Phillips's idea was, in his own words, "The Revival of the Derby China Manufacture." (11) It is easy to understand how the spark of this idea could ignite in the imagination of a man in Phillips's state of mind. But potential backers would need to be persuaded. Was there room for another fine china company? And why at Derby? Certainly Phillips and Litherland, each with a lifetime of experience and achievement in the industry, were in a better position than most to answer these questions authoritatively.

The history of Derby Porcelain in the 19th century contained one great irony.

On the one hand, the second and third quarters of the century had seen an unprecedented explosion of wealth in Britain as she led the world in the exploitation of the scientific discoveries of the industrial revolution. Not only was a new industrial aristocracy of millionaires rivalling the old landed nobility for power and wealth, but behind them a vast new middle class arose. Both groups constituted an enormous opportunity for purveyors of luxury goods, as long as those goods were designed to meet their taste.

On the other hand, in the same period the old Nottingham Road factory which had achieved such heights under the Duesburys, had declined and gone out of business. It had been replaced only by the small works at King Street, which a group of the potters had set up under the management of Sampson Hancock.

Phillips and Litherland could point to the progress made in this period not only by Worcester but by other firms, for example Minton which was not founded until the last years of the 18th century, but by good and imaginative management had come from nothing to premier position in the industry employing 1,500 workers and with an international reputation.

Now, in the latter part of the century, yet another opportunity presented itself in the form of the North American markets where untold fortunes were being made, and spent on objects of quality and beauty from Europe.

There was certainly room for a new competitor but why at Derby? A new porcelain factory at Derby could inherit from Duesbury a ready-made decorative tradition and reputation for quality. Furthermore Derby had the great advantage that while it was not in the Potteries, that great amorphous pool of ceramic skills and knowledge, it was less than an hour away by train.

However, it is time to introduce more members of the cast. First, William Bemrose, of the famous Derby printing firm.

William's father, also called William had come to Derby in 1815 and subsequently set up his business close to the Midland Railway headquarters. (12) Much of the work of the firm was for the railway, another growth industry, and the intelligent use of new technology for printing vast numbers of tickets, timetables,

WILLIAM BEMROSE

posters etc., provided the family with a growing fortune and reputation. William senior sold the ownership of the business to his two sons, Henry Howe and William junior in 1858. In Marilyn Swain's words, William Bemrose was "a typical product of the Victorian moneyed middle class: committed to the firm which produced his wealth, prominent in local affairs, but still with sufficient leisure to pursue in depth the subjects in which he was interested." Henry Howe Bemrose, the elder brother, devoted most of his surplus energy to politics, becoming mayor of Derby and for a time its member of parliament. William's interest lay in Art and Literature, and took his company into the publishing of journals such as "The Reliquary" an archaeological

16

quarterly whose first editor was Llewelyn Jewitt, also author of the Ceramic Art of Great Britain. In 1870 William himself had written and published, together with Alfred Wallis, "The Pottery and Porcelain of Derbyshire", and had started upon his highly distinguished career as a china collector. (At his death, his collection contained over 500 pieces of the highest quality.)

Here was an energetic influential Derby businessman, in his mid-forties, with a passionate interest in ceramics. Phillips's and Litherland's idea would naturally have tremendous appeal to such a man.

Next onto the stage comes John McInnes. He was a Scotsman, aged 65, with a highly successful career behind him as a chemist and manufacturer of enamel paints in Wallasey, Cheshire, which is of course just across the Mersey from Liverpool. According to his obituary "among his private researches, that in connection with paints for ships' hulls was a favourite. He experimented for many years in order to find a paint that could withstand the influence of sea voyaging, and ultimately success crowned his efforts. He then

JOHN McINNES

patented the material which became known throughout the shipping world and is now very widely used." (13)

John McInnes, as a senior figure in Liverpool life will have known William Litherland. Perhaps, too, he had come into contact with Edward Phillips many years before, when Phillips was in the enamel colour business himself. Whatever the truth of this, here was a very wealthy man, who would become convinced and excited by Litherland's and Phillips's argument, and would resolve to back their enterprise. Besides his commercial motive, and besides his intellectual interest in fine china, to which knowledge of chemistry is central, (14) he had another

17

important motive. He was anxious to find a place in business for his bright and ambitious son Edward.

The last important member of the group of founders of the company was Henry Litherland. Henry was William's young nephew, the son of his brother Thomas who was another china and glass retailer, in Ashby just 12 miles from Derby. Thomas himself appears not to have involved himself in the project at all, except that his shop was an early customer of the factory.

HENRY LITHERLAND

His son however became a major shareholder. Henry was slightly older than Edward McInnes, but they were both in their twenties. They became flat-mates (15) and eventually Edward was Henry's best man, (16) so clearly they were close friends. The two boys, who were to go into the new business as trainee managers, were both to play a crucial role in its development.

But let us go back to early February 1875, and to Edward Phillips, newly released from the service of Royal Worcester. The historian is presented with something of a problem: the records of the Company do not begin until its first meeting two years later in February 1877. So many of the events leading up to the start-up of the factory in 1878 have to be extracted from various sources, both from within the company archives and outside.

The contemporary accounts of the story of these three years are cursory, and go as follows: after leaving Worcester Messrs. Phillips and Litherland, joined by Mr. McInnes, first bought a plot of land next to the workhouse on Osmaston Road where they erected a sliphouse and mill; modelling began at rented premises; there were difficulties over planning permission; they then purchased the workhouse itself, formed a limited company, which converted the workhouse into a factory, and went into

18

production in spring 1878. (17) Not only is this account cursory, it also raises many questions.

First of all, who was involved, at what stage and in what form of association, to press forward with the project?

In the Company's share prospectus of 1877 we are told "it was at first intended that this undertaking should be commenced and carried on as a private partnership, consisting of three partners, Mr. Phillips, Mr. Litherland and Mr. McInnes." (See appendix III.) We do not know for sure if or when this partnership was formed, but we can see, from a set of accounts in our archive dated April 1877, who put up the first speculative money and when. Between August 1875 and April '77, William Litherland put up nearly £8,200. Edward Phillips put up just over £2,000 in the same period, but received back £750 in salary. John McInnes had contributed £700, however this was only just in the last month, March 1877. (18)

There are other clues to the financial arrangements of the partners. From Harry Frost's search of the Royal Worcester Minute Books, Litherland sold a block of Worcester shares in October 1875, but Phillips, who as we know had invested all he had in Royal Worcester, did not (perhaps could not) dispose of his shares until 1878. (It is curious that Litherland was actually buying preference shares in Worcester in 1878 to help finance their expansion scheme. So Litherland clearly had surplus cash to invest, and what is more was hedging his bets.)

Lastly, there is a note in the archive from McInnes to Phillips dated May '77 in which he writes "My Dear Phillips, (Thank you for) yours of yesterday enclosing dividend warrant for £120 on Worcester Porcelain stock which I shall place to your credit." I take this to mean that Phillips was paying off a loan from McInnes. (19)

So to sum up, it seems clear that a partnership of Phillips and Litherland was set up in spring 1875; that they were joined by McInnes later, perhaps in late 1876 or early '77, when it became obvious that substantially more funds were needed; that Phillips, who was the driving force and was organising the project, had few funds to put into the business, all his assets being tied up in Worcester until 1878; and that it was Litherland's money, and subsequently McInnes's, which paid the bills.

The first big bill came very early on. In June 1875, even before Phillips had agreed his severance terms with Royal Worcester, the partnership bought "about an acre and a half of building land adjoining the Derby workhouse for £2,500." (20) Soon after this, on September 17th the Derby and Chesterfield Reporter informed its readers that a piece of land in Litchurch just beyond the workhouse had been purchased and that a new china manufactory was about to be erected there. The nearest map, in date, to this period is that of 1852, (21) and it shows clearly the plot of land they bought. At the lower end are gardens or allotments, and at the top, by Osmaston Road, there is a house, called Ladygrove.

According to the prospectus of the Company published nearly two years later, (22) they erected a mill, for grinding stone, bone and colours, and a sliphouse with other buildings. These were built at the lower end of the plot, over the gardens.

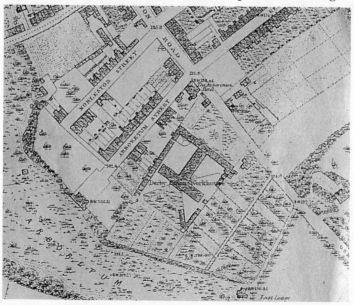

1852 MAP

(The solicitor's bill includes items for collecting rent and giving notice to quit to the garden tenants in early 1876.)

I had always assumed that the purchase of this plot was the first step in a plan to obtain the whole of the present site; but if so, they would have to have had very advanced notice of the sale of the workhouse for it did not take place until 18 months later. They would also have had to be sure of a successful purchase. A clue to the truth appears in the architect's first invoice. (23) An item back-dated to 1875, reads: "to 2½% commission on £5,202/0/0, remaining portion of Mr. Slater, the builder's original contract not executed through the purchase of the Union workhouse." It now is quite clear that there was a plan to build the whole factory on the Ladygrove site in what must have been a much less ambitious scheme than the final one. Hence the need to bring in new backers, primarily John McInnes, to finance the bigger scheme which only became possible when the opportunity to buy the workhouse presented itself.

There now began a period in which Edward Phillips's spirits must have swung from high excitement as step by step his dream came closer to realisation, to intense frustration as hurdle after hurdle appeared in his path, slowing up his progress and casting doubt over the whole project.

It seems that soon after the purchase of the Ladygrove site was agreed, Phillips moved to Derby, taking a house at number 64 Osmaston Road, just 17 houses away from Ladygrove towards the town. He appointed an architect E. L. Maddocks, of Hanley in the Potteries, a man who would be experienced in designing and adapting pottery factory buildings. The first item in Maddocks's first bill is dated August 1875, so they were clearly working on the detailed plans for a new factory on the Ladygrove site in the summer and autumn of that year. By November they had put the plans out to tender, asking builders for a quotation "to erect and complete the new china and earthenware manufactory in the Osmaston Road." Four quotations were received, two from the Potteries, one from Worcester, and the cheapest and successful tender not surprisingly was from a Derby firm, Slater. There were also quotations for boilers, for equipment for the mill, and for the sliphouse, for sinking a well and so on. Phillips was forging ahead as fast as he could to get into business.

However, at the end of October 1875 came the first set-back. On October 28th Phillips lodged the plans of his factory with the Litchurch local board for planning permission. (24) On the following day there was a meeting of the Board of Guardians of the Poor Law, owners of the workhouse which adjoined the Ladygrove site. It was revealed to them that Phillips was planning the construction of a china and earthenware factory immediately next door. Mr. Whiston, who was not only a solicitor and member of the Board of Guardians, but also occupied a villa on the other side of Ladygrove from the workhouse, (25) warned that the factory would emit noxious gases and objectionable smoke and pressed for the Board to protest to the planning authority. They had a further meeting on November 5th at which Mr. Whiston made a much more severe attack on the plan. Subsequently the Board of Guardians joined by another neighbour, the Arboretum committee, made representations to the Litchurch local board urging it to turn the plans down.

It is clear that Mr. Whiston's concern was that the factory would produce fumes such as those emitted by cheap earthenware factories using salt glazes, as was common in the Potteries. Phillips, of course, had no intention of producing such ware, but Whiston, who happened to be Clerk to the Litchurch local board, and his colleagues were not in a mood to be convinced.

The Litchurch local board met on November 12th and the Clerk to the Board revealed that he had asked for counsel's opinion in order to see whether the board had the legal power to prevent construction. The opinion was that it did not have such power, but that it would have the power to prevent the operation of the works after it had been built, as long as it could be proved that the factory was causing a nuisance. Counsel advised "that the local board should simply give formal notice to the persons

22

proposing to establish the works," that it would constitute the "establishing of a noxious or offensive trade, business or manufactory within the meaning of...The Public Health Act 1875."

Edward Phillips was present at this meeting and he was invited to speak. He made a spirited defence. The factory proposed at Derby was similar to his previous factory at Worcester and in a similar environment. The factory at Worcester was far from being a nuisance. "No fumes of any kind were thrown off," there was a little bit of smoke when the kilns were lit but after that, nothing. "Some of the finest gardens in the City of Worcester were near the china works and some of the finest crops of fruit grown in the country were also grown near them."

In spite of this, and in spite of the fact that it had no legal power to prevent construction as long as it complied with local bye-laws, the board passed a motion opposing the adoption of Edward Phillips's plan. But Phillips was not the sort of man to take no for an answer. He pursued his line of argument in the press, publishing a letter from the Worcester Medical Officer of Health, which confirmed that the Royal Worcester works were innocuous, and ended "I do not doubt that when your intended works are in operation, the good people of Derby will lose their fears, and welcome such a beautiful manufactory as an ornament and advantage to the town." (26)

Phillips also applied to his own counsel for advice, which was that he should ask again for permission since he ought not to commence building without the board stating that its bye-laws had been complied with. Phillips followed this advice, but the board simply replied by referring him to its original resolution. He then applied to the Queen's bench and obtained a decree nisi. The response of the board was extraordinary and very ill-judged; as Phillips wrote in a letter to the Derbyshire Advertiser, "when the affidavit of the board was put in opposition instead of being on the plea of expected injury to the surroundings, it was on the miserable subterfuge 'that the size and inclination of the drains had not been stated on the ground plan'...I cannot write my opinion of such conduct, as the architect...discussed the drainage arrangements...with the board surveyor and the understanding with him was, that the inclination of the drains should be as he desired when the levels had been taken...and that there was nothing in the plans he could object to." The furious Edward Phillips went on to say "all this unforeseen delay has caused me to entertain proposals for another business arrangement elsewhere, the building of the china works here will most probably be abandoned." (27)

Phillips's threat to take his china factory elsewhere hit a raw nerve in the community, and caused a furore. At this period, the cities of the Midlands were competing with each other for their share of the march of commercial progress; Derby had won the battle with Nottingham and Leicester to attract the Midland Railway Company, mainly because the other cities had been obstructive to the company's plans; the fruits of that victory in terms of prosperity for the town were abundant and clear for all to see. Now, the ratepayers of Litchurch saw a small clique of wealthy board members with exclusive villas in the vicinity of the proposed site, denying to the parish and indeed to the whole city the benefits of jobs, trade, contribution to the rates and the prosperity which would follow the establishment of an important new industrial concern. It was scandalous.

As it happened, a proportion of the members of the board were due to stand down and an election to replace them was to take place in April. In the run-up, the china factory became the overwhelming issue at stake. A public meeting, ostensibly "for the purpose of nominating candidates for the Local Board Selection," took place on March 22nd 1876. The hall was packed, and the newspaper account of the proceedings, complete with hecklers' interjections, makes the rowdiest modern House of Commons session pale in comparison.

First, the retiring members were obliged to give an account of their term of office; some tried to do so while avoiding mention of their role in the china factory issue, only to be greeted with cries of "How about the china factory?" and "How did you vote?" and "Hooting and hissing." One of them, the unfortunate Mr. Roe, tried to explain the board's position, only to be greeted with "What are you wasting time for, we shall be here till midnight?" Then finally the crowd shouted for Mr. Bemrose to speak.

William Bemrose was Vice Chairman of the Litchurch Board. At this point in the story, he had not yet met Phillips but he had voted against the board's rejection of Phillips's plan. Furthermore, at a later board meeting, he had criticised their handling of the issue, calling it "not quite straight forward and honest" for which comments the board had rounded on him. Now he made a speech which undoubtedly propelled him into the chairmanship of the board a month later, but which, considering that he declaimed it only feet away from his board colleagues on the platform, must have been dramatic and devastating.

First, he held up a white china-stone plate and declared "this was sent to me by a friend of Mr. Phillips this morning just to show you what it was they were going to manufacture. It will not hurt you if they manufacture 10,000 tons of it." He admitted to being the culprit board member who used the word "dishonourable"; now, he described the board's treatment of Phillips as a "dirty trick." "It was preposterous" he said "for a local board to say that a man should not build a manufactory because some day it might become a nuisance. The gentlemen who sat round the board should have met Mr. Phillips in a different spirit. Let us have smoke, trade and prosperity...The fumes would be...entirely consumed...before they got out of the top of the oven. Through this fallacy they had missed £200 or £300 a week in wages, ...and a new trade in the township. What is Derby famous for?...For its silk manufacture and its porcelain...The

25

name of Derby was known all the world over. They had an opportunity to revive this manufacture, but it had gone. Why? From the miserable paltry action of their local board." He sat down to thunderous applause and it was then moved that "In consideration of the treatment Mr. Phillips had received at the hands of a majority of the Litchurch local board, this meeting...expresses a hope that he will proceed at once with his works, instead of selecting another town." The resolution was passed with only one dissentient.

Later, the Derby Reporter commented: "Never...has an election in the district been so exciting...A number of the candidates...have issued printed addresses...setting forth their views...with regard to the china factory. Large posters have been placed upon the walls, requesting electors to vote for a certain candidate because they are in favour of trade and progress and have pledged themselves to favour the erection of the china works."(28)

In the next month a new set of pro-china works board members was elected, who in turn elected William Bemrose as Chairman; and most likely, with the special task of pacifying Mr. Phillips and persuading him to stay in Derby. A year later, the board was abolished and Litchurch became part of the Borough of Derby.

The newspaper reports of these controversial meetings cast light unexpectedly on two aspects of our story.

First, it had been believed that William Bemrose was responsible for encouraging Phillips and Litherland to come to Derby but this was clearly not the case. At the February meeting of the Litchurch board, when he strongly criticised the board's opposition to Phillips's plan, he stated quite categorically that "he did not know Mr. Phillips, never having seen him, neither was he personally interested in the matter." He repeated this statement at the raucous ratepayers' meeting in March. However he certainly met Phillips soon after this meeting; Phillips most probably will have wanted to thank him for his support and Bemrose will have wanted to encourage him not to leave Derby.

In any case he was very shortly to become an interested party.

Secondly, from the newspaper reports it is clear that it was by now public knowledge that sooner or later the workhouse was to be offered for sale. This fact would put the partnership into a considerable quandary. On the one hand, the Ladygrove site of 1½ acres was big enough to construct only a modest sized enterprise. The buildings would have to be constructed right against the boundaries, and there would be no room for anything but the factory – no cottages for the craftsmen most of whom would have to be enticed to come to Derby from the Potteries – no leafy gardens, no commodious roadways such as Phillips envisaged in his dream factory.

The acquisition of the workhouse, however, would transform the scheme completely. The workhouse site was a further 2¾ acres, making 4¼ in total; not only was there room for the whole dream, complete with workers' cottages, managers' villas, gardens and so on, but the workhouse buildings with their large and spacious rooms were ready made studios and workshops. There was also plenty of land at the rear of the workhouse to construct the kilns and placing sheds which would be needed.

But how long would they have to wait? And what if they failed to acquire the site? Litherland and Phillips decided that the only thing they could do was to carry out whatever work was possible and which would be relevant to both plans, with or without the workhouse. Beyond that they would simply have to sit and wait. They decided that the original position for the mill and sliphouse at the rear of the Ladygrove site was right for either plan, so they went ahead with construction there in the spring of 1876.

It is my strong conviction that after Edwards Phillips's experience with Binns at Worcester, he promised himself never to encumber himself with an Art Director again, but to be his own. (29) He must have spent much of the long and frustrating year of 1876 considering the nature and composition of his first ranges, and working on a programme for the modellers. He was also, of course, considering the kind of decorative treatment for his first wares, but it is probable that he wanted to avoid the expense of employing a full decorating department until his clay-to-glost departments were functioning smoothly. Consequently the first sales would be almost all of whiteware, much of it dependant on sculptural quality for its value.

Phillips and Litherland also knew that well before their factory could be commissioned they must have a range of models, block-moulds and cases ready in store for the first production run of working moulds. This meant that they must assemble a team of modellers and mould makers and set them to work on a range of items.

By this time, the summer of 1876, Phillips had moved from 64 Osmaston Road to the house at Ladygrove, and he invited R. G. Morris to start modelling work in a room in the house. (30) However, he had no premises to house the whole team of modellers and mouldmakers which he required, and here his new acquaintance William Bemrose came to his assistance. In March of that year, Bemrose's company had purchased Hadfield's mill in Chetwynd Street down in the centre of town in the Cockpit Hill area, in order to accommodate its expanding business. They moved part of their lithographing department to the mill, (31) but there was space to spare, so Bemrose offered to let it to the partnership for modelling, blocking and casing.

In August 1876 Phillips assembled his team. In charge was Walter Rowlands Ingram. In the Royal Crown Derby Archive there is an undated unsigned contract in Phillips's handwriting outlining his terms and conditions. It is a 3 year contract with a basic salary of £300 per year, a bonus of £100 after the 2nd and 3rd year; the hours are 9 a.m. to 6 p.m. with 1½ hours for lunch, 9am to 1 p.m. on Saturdays, although he can work at his own studio by arrangement. In return, Ingram "undertakes to design and model such small wares and articles as may be required to the best of his ability, and also to train and instruct such pupil or pupils as...Edward Phillips may place under his charge." (32) £300 relates to Phillips's own basic salary of £500 and shows what a relatively high value was put on the work of the head modeller of a late 19th century china firm.

The requirement to train pupils is a typical and sensible Victorian arrangement. Ingram's first apprentice was H. Warrington Hogg, who was later to become the senior modeller and Assistant Art Director of the Company. (33)

We also find a contract with William Stephan dated August 30th 1876 in which he agrees to act as "Designer and Artificer for Pottery models and shapes" and be paid three guineas a week, i.e. about £164 a year. (34)

The other members of the team were Simpson, S. Bourne and H. Bourne who were modellers and Wood, a mould maker. They moved into Chetwynd Street at the end of August 1876, and the accounts show Phillips paying the first wages on behalf of the partnership – just £6 in August, £51/12/6 in September, £72/7/0 in October, £79 and £92 in November and December.

Let us return to the question of the workhouse. We do not know when Phillips and Litherland first learnt that it would be coming up for sale, although it was certainly mentioned in newspaper reports in November 1875. Nor do we know when they decided that they must try to buy it. The fact that they began building only the sliphouse and mill in the spring of 1876, would suggest that they were keeping their options open for the possibility of obtaining the extra site.

The minutes of the meetings of the Derby Board of Guardians (35) cast a good deal of light on the story. In October 1875, well before the Litchurch row, they received a letter from Phillips's solicitor, Mr. Eddowes, informing them that his client was about to erect buildings on adjacent land with lights overlooking the workhouse grounds, and asking the consent of the Guardians. They refused. In the next month, as we have seen, they were protesting about the china factory. However by next April 1876, the row with the Litchurch Board was over, and Phillips's solicitor and the Guardians met to establish precisely where the boundary between their respective properties lay. On June 13th the Clerk reported that this matter was resolved, but 3 days later, they received another letter from Eddowes.

"Sir, upon my interview with you on Monday last with reference to the boundary between the workhouse property and that of my client Mr. Phillips, you made the remark that the former property would shortly be in the market for sale. Mr. Phillips....is anxious to know whether your board is prepared to sell a small portion of the workhouse property immediately adjoining the workhouse fence. Mr. Phillips is induced to make this request as his land at the back is rather narrow."

The Guardians considered this letter and resolved "that Mr. Eddowes be informed the Guardians are not prepared to negotiate for the sale of any part of the present workhouse property...until such time as they are legally empowered by an order from the local government board to proceed with the sale of the whole of such property."

I suspect that Phillips knew perfectly well that eventually they intended to sell the workhouse, but that he simply wanted them to show their hand, without showing them his. Now he must force them into action as soon as possible, so he wrote to their clerk personally on June 27th.

"Dear Sir,

I have your letter to Mr. Eddowes stating the resolution of the Board of Guardians as to the sale of the lower part of the workhouse land in Osmaston Road.

I write to say that I shall be willing to tender for the purchase of the whole (of the property), on condition that possession would be given of, say, twenty to thirty yards of the land adjoining the Arboretum fence by the latter end of this year, and the remainder whenever the Guardians were prepared to surrender..."

The response of the board was to form a sub-committee to deal with Mr. Phillips.

It was ironic that the members of this board, who had been persuaded by Mr. Whiston that the china factory would provide a nuisance which would reduce the value of that property, were now provided by that self-same factory with an opportunity to achieve a high price at a time when they wanted to sell.

Within a week the committee was back and on July 4th recommended "that application be made to the local government board authorising sale by auction of the property."

The local government board granted that permission in October, and at the beginning of December an advertisement in the Derby and Chesterfield Reporter announced that an auction of the property would take place at the Royal Hotel in Derby on December 15th 1876 at 6 p.m.

What were Edward Phillips's real feelings as he went into the hotel together with Mr. Eddowes on that December evening? If his bid failed he had a well conceived if modest scheme which he and William Litherland would probably be able to finance themselves with the help of their bankers, without the involvement of any further investors. Just a few thousand pounds had already been spent, the remaining building costs were only £5,200, the equipment of the factory and the working capital to bring the business into positive cash flow might be another £20,000 making a total of perhaps £30,000 to £35,000. If his bid succeeded however, then the project would take far more capital, another £50,000 to £60,000, much more time and much more effort. Additional backers would have to be attracted, a complete new construction plan would have to be created; even planning permission would have to be reapplied for. In short the whole project would have to be restructured. A lesser man might well have opted for the less ambitious plan. But at the front of Edward Phillips's mind there stood his dream factory, and behind it lay the desire to outshine Binns and Royal Worcester. Only the acquisition of the workhouse site could bring all that into reality.

Mr. Eddowes's bill for December 1876 contains one short item: to "attending sale of property where same was knocked down to Mr. Phillips for £9,150 – 1 guinea."

The die was cast.

3. Creating a company, a factory and a business

*E*dward Phillips now had to throw himself into resolving a whole host of new problems. It was a daunting but thoroughly welcome change, for 1876 had been an exasperating year for him. First the Litchurch row, and then the uncertainty over the acquisition of the workhouse had temporarily blighted his plans. All he had been able to do had been to build the mill and sliphouse, sign on his modelling team and set them to work, and try to prepare the ground in order to be in a position to finance the larger workhouse scheme if he was successful at auction.

At Christmas 1876, therefore, he and William Litherland had to move quickly, for before long they would have a bill for £9,150 burning a hole in their pockets. They needed to resolve not only that problem, but they needed to put together a legal and financial structure which would carry the business forward for the next few decades. It was at this point I believe that John McInnes entered the story. There is a legend of a crucial first meeting at Liverpool, predating the first company meeting in Derby, and the company prospectus casts some light on what may have transpired:

"It was first intended that this undertaking should be commenced and carried on as a private partnership consisting of three partners, Mr. Phillips Mr. Litherland of Liverpool and Mr. McInnes of Wallasey near Birkenhead, but at the desire of one of the partners, who does not wish to withdraw any portion of his share, but for family reasons desires to limit his liability, it has been determined to register it as a limited company with a small number of proprietors."

These three gentlemen could provide the core of capital required, but for the new scheme substantial additional funds were needed. It would also be healthy for there to be local money in the concern, and in this of course William Bemrose will have been in a position to help. Eddowes, the solicitor's bill for February 1877 gives a glimpse of the search for additional backers:

To..."Attending Mr. Phillips as to Sir N. Wilmot having declined to take shares – 6/8d.." to..."attending (Messrs. Evans and Mr. Newton) putting the matter fully before them when they agreed to take an interest and shares conditionally and I was to see them when matters were more matured – 13/4d.." to "attending with Mr. Phillips on Messrs. Walter and H.Evans...discussing proposal of Company...when they both agreed to become shareholders and not directors...afterwards attending Mr. Newton when he agreed same terms." And so on.

They also decided to take out a mortgage on the freehold of the property, and they persuaded one of the richest of the local landed gentry, Sir Tonman Mosley (great-grandfather of the famous Sir Oswald) of Rolleston-on-Dove, to give them a mortgage of £10,000 at 4% per annum.

In the meantime Eddowes was instructed to draw up memorandum and articles of association and to issue a prospectus for the new company with application forms for shares.

By the end of March all this was completed and the new company held its first directors' meeting on the 9th April at William Bemrose's office at Midland Place, Derby, (36) with Litherland, Phillips and Bemrose present. First, William Litherland was elected Chairman of Directors, and it was then ordered that the following shares be allotted:

William Litherland – 20 shares, Henry Litherland (son of William's brother Thomas, who had a china shop in Ashby) – 20 shares, John Bostock Litherland (Henry's half brother who worked with his uncle in the shop in Liverpool) – 2 shares, John McInnes – 20 shares, Edward Phillips – 15 shares, William Bemrose – 1 share, Henry Howe Bemrose (William's brother) –

1 share, Henry Evans (of the local banking family) – 1 share, Walter Evans (his brother) – 1 share, Charles Newton (a local landowner, J.P., D.L., Lord of the Manor of Mickleover) (37) – 1 share, Frederick Robinson (a local architect, with offices in Friargate, Derby) – 1 share.

So we can see that of the partners, the Litherland family dominated with 42 out of 83 shares, and the original trio of Phillips, Litherland and McInnes between them had 77.

This meeting also confirmed the transfer of all the property and assets from the partnership to the new company, confirmed that the mortgage should be proceeded with when the purchase of the workhouse was completed, and authorised Edward Phillips to sign cheques on behalf of the Company. (38)

There was another commercial and legal matter of great importance which needed to be arranged and that was the question of a trade mark and backstamp.

The period after the 1851 exhibition had seen a vast proliferation of trade marks in every sphere of business, and their historic importance in the pottery industry was emphasised by the appearance of both Chaffer's and Jewitt's famous surveys of factories and their marks. However it was not until 1875 that the Trade Marks Registration Act was passed, and the Trade Marks Registry set up.

A trade mark now became the assignable property of its owner, and he could sue for infringement simply on the basis of a certificate of registration. Hitherto it had been possible, but very difficult, to prove that an infringer was using a "borrowed" mark with intent to mislead. (39)

Phillips and his colleagues would have attached great importance to registering the right trade mark; Bemrose in particular, with his bent for history, and his friendship with Jewitt, will have been keen. Since the whole idea of this enterprise was "The Revival of the Derby China Manufacture" (that was the title of their prospectus) the trade mark must contain the basic elements of the original Derby backstamps: most importantly the crown, but also the D. The link with the past was essential.

Here again, Eddowes's bill, with its detailed but dead-pan descriptions of tasks and charges, tells the story. First, in March 1877 they designed a backstamp, and took it to the Registrar for approval and registration, but in vain. As we read in Eddowes's bill: "Attending Mr. Phillips as to...the Registrar having declined what was proposed and conferring...6/8d." Why were they refused? Sampson Hancock, whose little works at King Street had been set up in 1848 out of the ashes of the original Great Nottingham Road factory, had inherited from that business the right to use the mark of the crown, crossed swords and D. Clearly the Registrar was concerned that the new company's proposal was too close to that. So it was decided that Phillips should go and see old Mr. Hancock, simple soul that he was, and persuade him to assign to The Derby Crown Porcelain Company the right to use his mark or a variant of it. Mr. Hancock was most agreeable, but there was one small point: his mark was not registered either. Never fear, Mr. Phillips would see to all that and at his own expense. Mr. Eddowes set to work to prepare Hancock's application, as well as a declaration and an agreement assigning to Phillips the rights he wanted.

Then we read "Attending with Mr. Phillips on Mr. Hancock on his signing application to register and attesting his signature...6/8d" and "The like, declaration...6/8d. The like, Agreement, when he objected to one of the clauses, same struck out and attesting...6/8d."

Back they went to the Registrar, and back came Hancock's mark duly registered. But then things went seriously wrong; Mr. Hancock had brought in a solicitor, a Mr. Hextall, who first asked to be shown a copy of the agreement, and then informed them that his client now had objections to their using his trade mark, after all.

What could be done? Time was passing quickly, 4 months had elapsed already. They wrote to the Registrar for help, but in vain. They wrote again to Mr. Hextall pleading for a deal, but no reply. Mr. Phillips told Mr. Eddowes to try and visit Hextall in his office to find out what could be done, so another item reads "Attending Mr. Hextall but he was going away and desired the matter to stand over...3/4d." Phillips insists therefore that they must try and see Mr. Hancock himself, and an appointment was made, but then we read "Attending Mr. Phillips as to appointment and arranging another time...3/4d." If there was ever a case of stonewalling tactics, this was it. By now they were into September, and Phillips in an advanced state of exasperation.

Then, at last came some sort of breakthrough. On 11th September Mr. Eddowes received a letter from Mr. Hextall.

"Dear Sir,

Hancock & China Co.

Without prejudice, Mr. Hancock authorises me to lay before you the following alternative propositions the acceptance of either of which will be taken as a settlement of the questions which have arisen:

1. The Company to pay Mr. Hancock £10 – the agreement to remain in force (or another to be substituted for it at the cost of the Company if they prefer) the Company undertaking to use no portion of the trade mark other than the crown.

2. The agreement to be cancelled, each party remitted to their original rights no claim being made on Mr. Hancock for any expenses incurred by the Company as to registration." (40)

So Phillips must now devise another mark incorporating Hancock's crown, and they must persuade the Registrar to allow it. However that was not so simple: "Attending Registrar of trade marks, Long conference as to your being able to use the crown... 13/4d." (long indeed) "Writing Registrar with proposed trade mark...3/6d." "Conferring as to use of trade mark, the Registrar having declined to register the one proposed...6/8d." The most likely explanation of this is that the Registrar felt that the right to use the crown on its own could not be assigned, and that if it was then used in conjunction with other elements resembling

36

Hancock's and Duesbury's marks it remained an infringement. Happily, Phillips had not yet paid over the £10, so they were back, knocking at Mr. Hextall's door. Hancock must be persuaded to grant them the right to use the whole of his mark. It was not that they wanted to copy his mark; indeed their proposed mark was quite distinctive. But only by the acquisition of this right could they avoid a charge of infringement, and achieve registration.

Another exasperating two or three weeks elapsed, and then on 11th November, Eddowes dropped Phillips a note saying that Hextall and Hancock were prepared to settle. (41) "Attending Mr. Hextall on his stating that he was now prepared to settle the matter...3/4d." "Writing to Mr. Phillips for cheque for £10...3/6d and attending afterwards on Mr. Hextall, taking up grant, paying over £10 and settling....6/8d."

So finally the matter was resolved, and not a moment too soon, for only two months later the first finished pieces were coming into the new factory warehouse.

The final irony of this little saga was that compared to the £10 Phillips paid to Sampson Hancock for the rights he so desperately needed, Eddowes's total charge for helping him to acquire it was £19.

It is perhaps worth speculating on Sampson Hancock's view of the Osmaston Road enterprise. In the circumstances he seems to have been remarkably relaxed about what he might well have considered a major threat and intrusion. The new factory was laying claim to a pedigree which by rights was his, they were using one of the names by which his business was known, (both Crown Derby and Derby Crown were used for King Street) (42) they were likely to compete for his labour, (he lost one of his best artists, James Rouse, to Osmaston Road) and they would be using styles and designs which he had inherited from Nottingham Road.

And yet his reaction seems quite mild. John Twitchett quotes, in his book Royal Crown Derby (p.15), the letter which Hancock wrote to the Derby Reporter the week after it announced the plan to revive the art of china making in Derby. His letter politely points out the error, since his factory is evidence that the art has never died. There is no hint of antagonism to the project. Later, when Phillips approached him he seems to have been prepared to sign an agreement over the backstamp without asking for anything in return, and it was only when he introduced his own solicitor that the two of them became more demanding; but even then, £10 seems a relatively small sum for such a precious right. There is proof in the Osmaston Road sales journal that relations between the two businesses were amicable: as early as July 1878 there are invoices for firing ware for Hancock, and in December of that year they supplied Hancock with biscuit ware decorated with blue bands. (43)

Yet there must have been some resentment, and a hint of it appears in a newspaper interview with Hancock in 1895. Hancock describes the Japan ware, and the "grotesque patterns such as Dr. Syntax, the Mansion House dwarfs, etc." which his firm manufactured. Since Osmaston Road also manufactured them, the interviewer's next question is a loaded one: "I expect that you suffered a good deal from counterfeit ware masquerading as your own?" – "Yes we have been and still are the victims of unprincipled makers. The subject of marked monograms is, however a big one ......" Little did the interviewer know. (44)

Let us go back to the early part of 1877. By this time Edward Phillips had decided on the final plan for the Derby Crown Porcelain factory. The share prospectus describes in detail what had been done and what was intended.

"The mill and sliphouse have already been erected and a fifty horse power engine is being installed. Ovens and kilns are now being erected on the workhouse land, and "if full possession of the buildings and other parts of the site can (as promised) be retained early in the summer, it is hoped that...the business of the company may be commenced in the autumn of the present year."

"The services of a gentleman of high class reputation as a

sculptor and modeller have been secured...other modellers and mould makers have also been...at work in premises rented at workshops."

"It is intended at once to commence building twenty residences...for the manager, artists and other principal employees. The area of the first land purchased which is not built upon and will not be required for the works, will be ample for the purpose."

"The front of the present workhouse buildings will be rebuilt and converted into a handsome elevation, containing extensive showrooms open to visitors and the open space in front will be laid out ornamentally with a spacious carriage approach to the front entrance."

It seems possible that it was at this moment that Phillips commissioned the well-known engraving, a bird's eye view of the factory of his dreams, so similar to the one he had produced at Worcester, back in 1863. (see illustration p.54)

However, all these confidently announced plans were to prove much more difficult to realise than to describe in a prospectus.

The first obstacle was the continuing occupancy of the inmates of the workhouse. Phillips had succeeded in persuading the Guardians to put the workhouse up for sale earlier than they would otherwise have done, but it soon became clear that they were not going to complete the sale, nor vacate the building, before they were ready to move the inmates to a new workhouse.

Phillips's short term objective, however, was met, and that was to be able to use part of the land and buildings at the back of the workhouse. A week after the auction, on December 19th the Board of Guardians met again and resolved "That Mr. Phillips be granted possession of land (a part of the infirmary airing grounds)...with necessary access upon his fencing same off to prevent communication with the inmates of the workhouse.."

Even if he did not yet have possession of the whole site, at least he now knew exactly where he was going. The first task was to fit out the mill and sliphouse buildings which Slater the

39

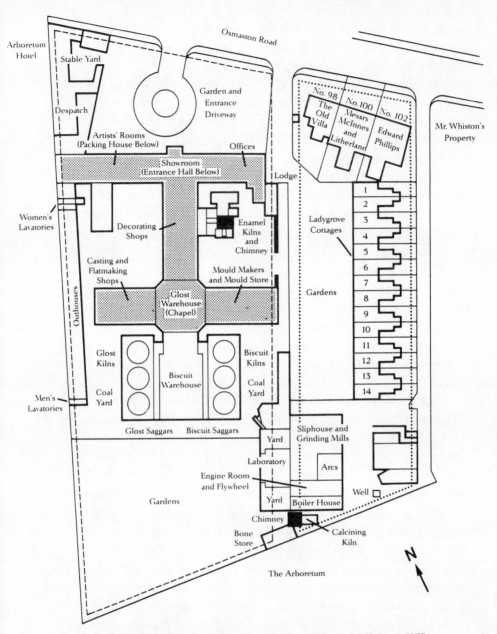

Osmaston Road

Arboretum Hotel

Stable Yard

Despatch

Garden and Entrance Driveway

Artists' Rooms (Packing House Below)

Offices

No. 98 The Old Villa

No. 100 Messrs McInnes and Litherland

No. 102 Edward Phillips

Mr. Whiston's Property

Showroom (Entrance Hall Below)

Lodge

Women's Lavatories

Decorating Shops

Enamel Kilns and Chimney

Ladygrove Cottages

Casting and Flatmaking Shops

Mould Makers and Mould Store

Glost Warehouse (Chapel)

Gardens

Outhouses

Glost Kilns

Coal Yard

Biscuit Warehouse

Biscuit Kilns

Coal Yard

Men's Lavatories

Glost Saggars   Biscuit Saggars

Sliphouse and Grinding Mills

Yard

Laboratory

Arcs

Engine Room and Flywheel

Yard

Well

Gardens

Boiler House

Chimney

Bone Store

Calcining Kiln

N

The Arboretum

1
2
3
4
5
6
7
8
9
10
11
12
13
14

········· Boundary of Ladygrove property, purchased by Litherland and Phillips in 1875

– – – – Boundary of Board of Guardians' property, purchased 1876

▦▦▦▦ Extent of original workhouse building in 1876

builder had erected, with all the necessary plant and equipment, and to extend them on the workhouse side so that they could service the whole of the new and larger factory.

For most of the equipment he engaged the engineering firm of George Barker although he bought a steam engine from Abell of Derby. However it was powered by a boiler from Barker and it drove Barker's machinery including a great flywheel with cogs and gears, which operated 6 large grinding pans on the first floor for stone, bone and glaze frit, and six smaller pans for colours in the next room. The body materials from the pans, mixed in a "blunger" with water pumped from a well 22 yards deep sunk in the yard outside, was washed down through sieves to storage "arcs" sunk into the floor of the building; from there it was either to be taken in tubs to the casting shops or pressed and put through a pug mill in the sliphouse on the ground floor, ready for flatmaking. (45)(see plan of works opposite)

Next to the sliphouse was the bone store, bone crushing machinery, and a calcining kiln for both bone and flint, built by the Stoke firm of Windsor. The firm of Matthews was engaged to erect a massive chimney servicing the boiler and calcining kiln.

Next to that was the laboratory, most important for the testing and quality control of materials, and of course for experimentation with colours glazes and bodies. It was here that John McInnes came when he visited the works, and here that Tom Hough, the Company's chemist, worked under old Mr. McInnes's inspiration. (46) According to a contemporary description the lab was constructed out of the "fever hospital" of the old workhouse. (47)

Unfortunately, things did not go smoothly with George Barker on this part of the site. When his men came to install the great flywheel which was to be positioned vertically against the wall of the engine house, they dropped it and it cracked. The crack was repaired by plating but, as Phillips wrote to Barker "How am I to be secure against any other injury to the wheel from the fall? From the slovenly way the machinery has been put together any slight crack would be passed over and may

41

ultimately cause the wheel to break down. If you have any misgivings as to the cracked driving wheel lasting two years you had better replace it with a sound wheel." Phillips withheld payment until Barker signed a legal document guaranteeing it for two years on pain not only of replacing the wheel but of reimbursing all damage done by the breaking of the wheel, to be assessed by independent auditors. Not for the first time did Edward Phillips reveal himself as a tough customer. (48)

Happily George Barker's guarantee was unnecessary, and at least one former employee remembers the great wheel driving the mill and sliphouse machinery effortlessly sixty years or so later. (49)

As we have seen from the prospectus, Phillips expected to have possession of the workhouse in early summer and hoped to be in production in the autumn, but this turned out to be far too optimistic. The Guardians refused to proceed at any but the most sedate pace, and Eddowes was instructed several times to try and hurry them up: once more, his bill paints the scene.

May: "attending Mr. Phillips as to completion and time of getting possession...writing to Mr. Shaw (of the Board of Guardians)...thereon...attending Mr. Phillips again as to possession."

June: "writing to Mr. Shaw to return draft conveyance approved...writing to him again to same effect...attending Mr. Phillips as to getting possession...attending Mr. Phillips again on his urging necessity for early completion...and writing to clerk of Board of Guardians...writing to Mr. Watson (another Guardian) as to when possession could be given...attending Mr. Shaw conferring as to completion.

July: "writing to Mr. Shaw as to.... whether Mr. Phillips could go over premises to check inventory... attending Mr. Phillips as to inspecting premises and completion...."

The process was dragging on and on. One minor problem was resolved, namely that the modellers down at Chetwynd Street were running out of space to store the models, blocks and cases they were producing. On April 10th the Board of

Guardians resolved to allow Phillips to use a room in the workhouse for their storage. But for the rest, Phillips was becoming more and more exasperated at their delays.

Finally in mid July, a full eight months after the auction, the lawyers completed, the balance of the purchase price was paid, the deeds were handed over and sent as mortgage security to Sir Tonman Moseley, and by the end of the month, Phillips had possession. (50) The modelling team left Chetwynd Street and installed themselves in the empty building on August 3rd 1877. (51)

From this point onwards, right up until the summer of 1880, the site at Osmaston Road must have been in varying degrees of chaos. Several teams of builders were at work, engineers, plumbers, painters and decorators, kiln builders; and in addition to this, hands were being taken on to produce china, gradually filling up the workshops as they became available for use.

The conversion of the workhouse building was relatively simple. It was a curious, large and gaunt building in the shape of an H, the verticals of which ran parallel to the Osmaston Road. In the centre of both wings at the point where they were joined by the connecting range there was a dome. We are not sure what the Osmaston Road front of the old workhouse looked like, except that there was a large vaulted eating hall in the centre lit by the front dome. Behind this, the buildings had 3 stories, except under the back dome, where the second and third levels were occupied by a round chapel. From the apex of this chapel hung a large brass bell. Apart from the front range, where the rooms were connected by a passage at the back, the buildings had a narrow central passage serving workshops or rooms to left and right. The floors were reached by a series of narrow staircases, some of them spiral. (see plan of works, p.40)

While the rooms made an ideal series of workshops the staircases and passages were by no means ideal and rather narrow for carrying wareboards and the like. If two people met on one of the spiral staircases, one of them had to press himself into a doorway to let the other pass.

All that needed to be done in the workhouse was to equip these rooms as a series of workshops and process warehouses. The chapel became a glost warehouse (known as "the ring"), the chapel bell was used to announce opening and closing time; the lodgeman would let nobody out of the gates until the bell had been rung. The cellars were used for the storage of clay, and the kitchen was converted into a throwing room. (52)

The main thing which needed to be added, of course, was the facility for firing, and the kilns would have to be positioned in accordance with the flow of work-in-progress through the factory site. Phillips's and Maddocks's scheme was that it should flow diagonally across the site from the mill and sliphouse at the south corner by the Arboretum, to the packing house at the north corner with access to Arboretum Street. The making and glazing shops were therefore in the rear workhouse wing, nearest the sliphouse, and so they decided to build two rows of three kilns, one for biscuit and one for glost firing, at the back next to the rear wing. Between these rows was a large biscuit warehouse, leading off the circular chapel building.

The decorating or enamel kilns needed to be to the front of the building near the decorating shops but where there was much less space to accommodate them. What was required was a larger number of smaller kilns which could be fired separately to cater for the variety of ceramic colours used, which matured at different temperatures. In the west yard they built a remarkable complex which consisted of seven kilns, in an oblong configuration. Above the oblong there arose a massive 150 foot chimney stack which took the fumes from these kilns way up above the sensitive heads of the citizens of Litchurch. Beneath this stack was a large archway, so that there was access to the kiln sheds from inside as well as from outside in the yard.

A bewildering number of companies were brought in to erect and equip all of this:

Matthews built the chimneys; Slater built the mill, sliphouse and engine house; Brookes built the oven cones; Walklate built the ovens; Walley built the boiler; Windsor built the enamel

44

kilns; Skevington provided the plumbing; Stacey Davies provided cast-iron roofs; Bakewell built sheds

With all of these at work on the site simultaneously, it must at times have seemed like pandemonium.

The first priority of the directors was to achieve a working china factory, but the prospectus had described two further objectives: the building of twenty residences and the handsome re-fronting of the building, with elegant showrooms behind, and gardens and carriageway in front.

Phillips obviously attached great importance to the building of the residences, correctly foreseeing great difficulty in attracting skilled labour from the Potteries and, perhaps, from Worcester.

He also wanted one of the residences for himself. His first address, as we have seen, was 64 Osmaston Road but it only occurs in the very early correspondence of 1875. In 1877 and '78, those letters not addressed to the china factory itself, are addressed to "Ladygrove," (53) and a newspaper article also confirms that he was living in the small villa of that name which came with the original site. (54) At the time of the Litchurch row he was still sending some of his letters from his address in Malvern, but it seems probable that once the row was over and a factory was certain to be built, he closed his Worcestershire establishment to settle permanently in Derby, bringing with him his Worcestershire-born housekeeper Mrs. Everett. (55)

In this case, as before, the prospectus was optimistic: twenty residences turned out in fact to be only fourteen cottages and two villas, which together with the original Ladygrove villa made a little terrace of three fronting onto the Osmaston Road. It is difficult to say whether the cottages really were important in recruiting and keeping good employees. The 1881 census recorded 25 residents who certainly were employees, and three (a labourer, house painter and clerk) who probably were, making 28 out of a total labour force of about 300. The residents were for the most part skilled, potters, painters, firemen and so on, but in number they do not appear so significant.

45

What is certain is that these residences were one of the most expensive items to be met by the shareholders' capital. Bakewell's building firm won the contract to complete the job for £5,630. (56)

Furthermore, money was beginning to be a problem. The urgency to start producing and selling goods, to provide an inflow of funds and begin to counteract these growing outflows was uppermost in Phillips's mind. He was questioning every quotation and every bill. We have already read of the dispute with Barker over the damaged wheel, and Barker, at one stage in the correspondence accused him of playing for time. In November the directors met and agreed that the bill from Mr. Maddocks, the architect was excessive; Maddocks offered a reduction, which the directors rejected, and he finally offered a larger reduction of £86, off a bill of £461. Poor Mr. Eddowes the solicitor had the same treatment; the directors considered that his charge of £100, a 1% commission on the mortgage with Sir Tonman Moseley, was excessive, Mr. Bemrose's view was that it was "at least double what it should be." Eddowes, never one for a round number, deducted £25/4/10.

The great pipeline of work-in-progress gradually filled up over the autumn and winter of 1877 and '78, and as it did so the workshops filled with operatives. The first of these, of course, were the modellers and mould makers, who arrived on August 3rd. (57) By December the first biscuit kiln full of ware was ready to fire; strangely enough we learn this from the archive at Minton, whose patented down draught kiln design Phillips chose to use for two biscuit kilns.

Leon Arnoux, the great art director and technician of Minton had invented the down draft oven, the purpose of which was much greater efficiency of fuel consumption, and greater cleanliness of waste fumes. In this revolutionary kiln, the fumes from the fire travelled not as before through an aperture in the roof, but met a solid roof and were redirected back down through apertures in the floor of the kiln, and then out through a series of flues to the chimney above.

46

Arnoux came over to Derby to advise on the dimensions and design of the kilns and in December, after his visit, Phillips wrote asking him to test some Derby-made saggars in the Minton kilns, and also enquiring if it would be possible to borrow a fireman to conduct the first biscuit fire at Derby. Arnoux replied:

"Your saggars are arrived and they will be returned to you towards the end of next week. We could not spare our china biscuit fireman, as we have only one, and it would be impossible for him to go to Derby between the firings; but if you could manage to have your oven fired during Christmas week, then he might go. We think that it would be worth for you to make your arrangements accordingly."

Phillips replied saying that Christmas week would suit him well, and on the December 19th wrote again "...I find the first china biscuit ovens will be ready for your fireman on Friday 28th." (58) So Minton's biscuit fireman missed his Christmas week break that year; and in January the Company paid a bill for £186, representing £10 per annum per kiln for nine years and 4 months in advance. (59)

It was not until six weeks later, after that first biscuit fire, in Christmas week 1877, that the first finished ware was taken from the enamel kilns. In William Bemrose's personal collection there was an item described as a "porcelain jug, white and gold with inscription: 'one of the first dozen manufactured at the Crown Porcelain works, Derby: February 7th 1878'." An historic jug indeed. (60)

During the month of February goods were being assembled in the warehouse ready for despatch, and in the factory sales journal the first sale is recorded on 2nd March, appropriately enough to the Company's own Chairman William Litherland, of one white china sea horse shell, and a cupid shell dolphin. The second despatch, of two pairs of white china Derby dwarfs, went to Thomas Goode in South Audley Street, London, and the third and substantial order of some 40 pieces of white and ivory sculptural and ornamental pieces went off to Edward Phillips's cousins W. P. & G. Phillips for their famous china and glass emporium in Oxford Street London.

The ship was launched, but it was to be some time before she could be said to be properly under way. It appears from the sales journal that it was not until May that quantities of fully decorated ware were despatched. These first despatches were divided between relatively small quantities of sculptural items, sent to the major china and glass retailers, and quite large quantities of earthenware tableware, most of which for some reason at first went to J. B. Edwardes of Folkestone (probably a catering trade wholesaler). After two or three months however, decorated ornamental and useful ware began to appear, and the items sold became well balanced between white and ivory bone china and earthenware, and between ornamental and useful ware. The first export order to Tiffany's of New York went out in August.

Phillips and his colleagues now had a very substantial factory to keep busy and although all their pronouncements to the public emphasised the high quality and artistic aspirations of their enterprise, they realised perfectly well that they would not survive by producing expensive art objects and nothing else. Their objective was to establish a reputation for the highest quality, by employing the finest artists and craftsmen, and linking their efforts to the glories of the past, but at the same time to use that reputation to sell considerable quantities of less expensive and everyday china, not only to the general public but also to the catering trade. Indeed, hotels and hotelware distributors were among their first customers. The early catalogues illustrate well their "crown" earthenware ranges of tea sets at reasonable prices, many of them decorated in the Japan style, many of them using the "print and tint" technique to give plenty of colour for little cost. (61)

Nevertheless, it was extremely important to recruit and retain some of the finest ceramic artists including, if possible one or two international stars, and here William Litherland with his European contacts could help. Early in 1878 he approached Georg Landgraf who was working at the Konische Porzellan Manufaktur in Berlin, and persuaded him to come to Derby. (62)

They also succeeded in attracting Count Holtzendorf, and these two artists, of stature and reputation, shared a studio which became a regular and important stopping point for visitors and journalists. (63) In addition, Phillips persuaded John Porter Wale his former employee at Worcester to come to Derby as head painter, supervising a team of artists of the second rank. (64)

Meanwhile, as the work of bringing the factory physically into being progressed, the Board of Directors were also concentrating on the legal and financial aspects of the business.

The first directors, elected at that first meeting in William Bemrose's office, were William Litherland Chairman, Edward Phillips Managing Director, and Bemrose himself. The factory at this time was under construction and not the sort of place to hold board meetings, and the next one, a general meeting, took place at No. 4 Albert Street in the centre of Derby, Eddowes's office and the Company's temporary registered office, on July 7th. At this meeting John McInnes was also elected a non executive director. McInnes and Litherland of course both lived on Merseyside, and it must have been extremely useful to Edward Phillips to have at least one fellow director, Bemrose, to hand in Derby with whom to discuss matters. Until May 1878 when the factory was ready to accommodate board meetings, Bemrose and Phillips had to travel to Liverpool for meetings at the Adelphi Hotel. (65)

When the board met next, on August 9th 1877, Edward Rowell of Manchester was appointed as Company Secretary, which relieved Eddowes of his temporary role in this capacity. Rowell had a family connection with the Litherlands; his sister was married to John Bostock Litherland. (66) But it is also in the minutes of this meeting that we see signs that the project was going to require some substantial extra tranches of capital: Mr. Newton proposed that the Company take out an additional mortgage of £10,000 at 4½% or else a debenture at 5%. In the event the money was raised by a mixture of the two: Sir Tonman Moseley granted a further mortgage of £8,000 at 4½%, and two debentures of £1,000 each were issued at 5% and were taken up by John McInnes. (67)

The ordinary shareholders were also being called upon for funds. They were required to make a deposit of £20 per share upon allotment in April 1877, and the first call came in May, of £80 per share. By July of 1878 a further £200 per share had been called, and by the last call, in July 1881 another £150 had been required. So the total cost of an ordinary share was £450, and with 83 shares subscribed £37,350 was raised in this way. (68) The nominal share value was £500, and the original prospectus had stated that only three quarters of this sum would be required. Once again the prospectus proved over optimistic.

On Tuesday July 23rd Edward Phillips and William Bemrose met to go through the first year's accounts (their financial year ran from July to June). They instructed the new Secretary Edward Rowell to pass these accounts to the auditor, and to send the following report to each shareholder summarising the progress they had made so far, and which was adopted by the first A.G.M. on the following Friday.

Report of the Directors July 26th 1878.

"Your Directors present their first yearly report as to the progress made in the erection of ovens, kilns and other necessary new buildings on the land and premises purchased from the Poor Law Guardians of which they obtained full possession the latter part of July 1877.

"They have to report that the china biscuit ovens and placing houses are completed and have been in full operation since January last, – the cones for the three glaze ovens and placing houses, have been completed and two of the ovens built and found to work satisfactorily – the remaining oven will be built by the Company's bricklayer, to fill up spare time.

"Seven enamel kilns are completed of various sizes which will be sufficient for the business of the Company for some years, and the workshops required for the different departments are now fitted up and partly or wholly occupied.

50

"A few ornamental goods were sent out in March, and since decorators have been at work a steady increase of business in low priced ornaments was confirmed and satisfaction expressed by the dealers with the style and quality of the articles sent out.

"A good and sufficient stock of white china and crown ware has been got ready and your Directors expect to have patterns and goods ready for the dealers in the autumn, when they trust to have a fair share of the trade both home and foreign.

"Your Directors do not recommend the completion of the front elevation of the works until the wholesale trade is somewhat developed.

"They report to have found much more difficulty in obtaining steady competent hands than was expected but by degrees a better class of hands has been secured and in a few months many of the apprentices will be producing and finishing goods for sale.

"Your Directors have good hopes from the friendly feeling expressed by many of the dealers to have to report at the next Annual Meeting a very fair year's business for a new concern's first operations."

Now that the factory was in production, the Company needed a London showroom. Retailers in those days would place orders in spring for the summer season, and in autumn for the winter. The sales representatives would therefore undertake two sales journeys a year but there was a limit to the samples they could carry with them. Almost all substantial pottery manufacturers of the time therefore, had showrooms in London as well as at the factory, and in addition they would send showcase displays to important provincial exhibitions. (69) A London showroom was particularly important for those interested in the lucrative American trade, and more so for a factory outside the Potteries like Derby or Worcester, where an American buyer would find it difficult to make a special visit.

In August 1878 Edward Phillips travelled to London and

put up at the Salisbury Hotel, (70) just off Fleet Street, close to the area around Holborn viaduct where most china manufacturers had their showrooms. (Royal Worcester for example was in Charterhouse Street, just to the north of the viaduct). Perhaps his London cousins, William & George Phillips had done some homework on his behalf before his arrival but he found good premises to let at 27 Ely Place, and by the end of the month he had signed an agreement to rent them at £170 per annum. He also appointed a London agent Mr. Spiers (71) to look after them and manage the London trade and by October the London end of the business was in operation.

The other premises which interested Phillips were the houses he was building at Derby, particularly the one he had earmarked for himself, his housekeeper Mrs. Everett, and his maid. (72) The construction of the villas and cottages was completed in the summer of 1878, and after the painters and decorators had done their work, Phillips moved from the original Ladygrove villa, to the new villa at the other end of the terrace in mid September. It was not until the following year that the two boys, Edward McInnes and Henry Litherland moved into the middle house of the three, also with housekeeper and maid. At the same time Edward Rowell, the new Company Secretary, (and Henry's relative by marriage) with this young wife and new born daughter, moved into the old villa. (73)

There was one more major investment to be made. As the prospectus promised, "The front of the present workhouse buildings will be rebuilt and converted into a handsome elevation, containing extensive showrooms open to visitors, and the open space in front will be laid out ornamentally with a spacious carriage approach to the front entrance." However before the directors could embark upon this, they must raise a great deal more capital. The project planned was likely to cost around £2,000, but they needed to raise much more than that. When Phillips had drawn up the Company's prospectus in March 1877, he underestimated seriously, not only the time it would take to start up the business, but also the amount of capital it would require.

It seems most likely that while the estimates for constructing the factory were reasonably simple to calculate, and therefore accurate, it was impossible to estimate the working capital needed, particularly in stocks. By June 1880, for example, the value of finished stocks was over £15,000, and customers owed £4,700. The working capital was nearly as high as the fixed assets.

Once again we can detect Phillips's dogged and urgent determination behind the scenes. A lesser man (perhaps a wiser one) would not have grasped the opportunity to buy the workhouse, or would have postponed the building of the residences, and now, would have postponed the conversion of the front. But instead he persuaded his directors that the thing must be done properly and sooner not later. If more capital was required, more must be raised. In November 1878 a new prospectus was prepared for private circulation which read as follows:

"The...works are now in full operation and good orders are being received and executed. Premises have been taken and a depot and an agency established in London.

"The Directors now desire to complete the front of their works, on which will be constructed a showroom and rooms for the principal decorating and modelling artists, and to enable them to do this, they have decided to issue £10,000 six per cent preference stock at par; of this sum £5,000 has been subscribed by the two largest shareholders." (74)

The two large shareholders can only have been Litherland and McInnes; but in the event the issue was oversubscribed and brought in £10,500. (75) This issue was extremely generous: not only was 6% a high rate of return in those non-inflationary days, but it was payable in arrears, so that if one year the Company could not afford a dividend, the next year it must pay the preference shareholders twice, before ordinary shareholders received anything. This had a serious effect in the returns from, and therefore value of, ordinary shares. By the early 1900's these shares which originally cost £450 were changing hands at only £150 each. (76) The fact that in spite of this injection of capital, by 1880 the Company's overdraft at the bank was £2,648 (77) shows how badly the money was needed and explains the generosity of the terms; the money was needed not simply for refronting the workhouse but for working capital. The prospectus was not as explicit as it might have been on this point.

In the spring of 1879, Phillips was ready to proceed with the conversion. Maddocks, his architect from the Potteries was a specialist in china factory design and construction, but the task in hand was aesthetic rather than functional, and Phillips may well have wished to avoid the ponderous style of factory front so beloved of the Staffordshire Potters. (78) Furthermore one of the Company's shareholders, Frederick Robinson was an architect and it was he who produced the design and supervised the work on the new front. (79)

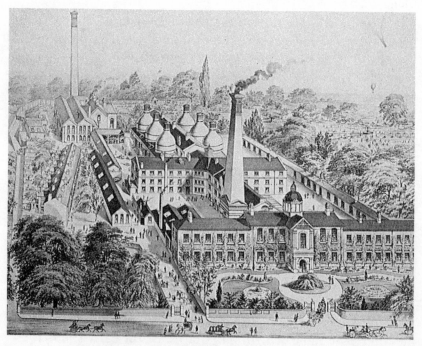

THE DREAM FACTORY

54

We have no illustration of the original front of the workhouse, so the nature of the external remodelling is not clear. The basic shape of the building as it appears on the 1852 map did not change, except for the central projecting portico, encased by classical pilasters. (80) The fenestration will have been altered to match, also the dome with a cast iron crown to cap it. Inside, there was no expense spared to create the impression of an enterprise of the first rank. The entrance hall · was tiled with Minton Hollins's best, and illuminated by windows and skylight glazed with stained glass by Swaine Brown. This led to an elegant stairway with cast iron balusters and newel posts, which in turn led into the showroom. (81) A visitor on one of the first Crown Derby factory tours in 1881 described it as follows:

"The last and perhaps the greatest treat in store for us was a visit to the magnificent showroom of the establishment. This is a noble apartment divided into two bays or transepts by a dome of considerable height, which throws a flood of light into the room and shows off the many delicate articles on view to the best possible advantage...In the centre plays a very pretty

fountain in the bowl of which a number of goldfish disport themselves with becoming gravity...Every intending china buyer ought to visit the room...we can promise them they would not be disappointed." (82)

However, even this part of the construction of Edward Phillips's dream went neither smoothly nor quickly. On May 5th 1879, Phillips and George Fryer the builder signed an agreement whereby the latter agreed to commence work on May 7th, and complete the whole on or before September 30th, on pain of forfeiting the sum of £5 per week thereafter until the work was completed. (83)

On December 12th Edward Phillips and William Bemrose travelled to Liverpool to meet their Chairman at the Adelphi Hotel. Phillips reported that "owing to the dilatory attention of the contractor the showroom is not yet roofed in or the walls plastered" and they agreed that the company should enforce the penalty. In the event they proposed to deduct £100 from the bill, which, when Fryer protested, they reduced to £80. (84)

In total the cost of building and fitting out the new showrooms and studios amounted to £1,848 (85) and it was not until the end of January that they were ready to place advertisements in the local papers announcing that the factory was open for visitors.

Delays with construction were not the only frustration during the years of 1879 and '80, for sales were slower to take off than was hoped. In order to start generating a surplus, and reverse the constant requirement for additional funding, sales needed to reach about £19,000 a year. In the first full financial year of operation, July to June 1878/9, sales had been nowhere near that level, at only £6,080. (86)

This was no more than could have been expected. The Directors' Report of that year bemoaned lost business caused by the need to stock up the London showroom and provide samples for the salesmen, thereby delaying the execution of orders. However, they had mounted displays at an exhibition in York and at another in Wakefield. They felt that they had established a favourable position in the market, and they were particularly pleased with the response from America, to which market invoiced sales of over £1,000 had been made and where they were experiencing substantial repeat business. The next year, 1879/80 showed a substantial sales increase to £14,530 but was still well short of the break-even point.

Nevertheless the Directors, in their report of August 1880, now "consider the capital of the Company virtually intact, and the deficiency will be turned into a balance of profit as soon as an improvement in the trade of the Company increases the returns."

There was one aspect of the business with which Edward Phillips must have been very pleased. The two boys, Edward McInnes, John's son, and Henry Litherland, William's nephew, were proving themselves as managers of the business. By 1880 they were both still in their twenties, Edward 23 (87) Henry 29 (88) and since Phillips had no suitable son nor heir, it was important for the long term that they should be trained for eventual succession. Furthermore, with both the two other major shareholders away on Merseyside it was important to Phillips that he and the boys form an executive team of three, which would help to take some of the weight off his shoulders. It was not unnatural that Henry, son of a retailer and nephew of another, should specialise in the commercial aspect, and that Edward son of a chemist and technical man, should be interested in production. (89) In November 1880, it was proposed that they should both join the board, and they were duly elected.

But alas, the weight on Edward Phillips's shoulders was becoming heavier not lighter. Cash flow remained a serious problem and there were two further calls on the ordinary shareholders, one in December 1880 and another in July 1881, each of £25 per share. Furthermore Phillips had become disenchanted with Mr. Spiers, the London agent, describing him as "very remiss in his duties." Spiers was given three months' notice in February 1881. (90) Worst of all, trade in general was slack. By the end of the financial year, sales had reached only £15,720, still well short of the £19,000 break-even point.

The Directors' Report on the year 1880/81 made fairly gloomy reading:

"...the operations of the Company have been carried on the last year under great and unexpected difficulties, partly from the misconduct of the Company's travellers and from having to dismiss dissolute workmen and replace them with other untried men.

"Owing to the continued depression of the home trade and having losses from bad debts...the returns for the last year have not increased as your Directors hoped and expected, and are not yet sufficient to yield a profit after paying working expenses.

"The number of customers on the Company's books is gradually extending, and should there be a revival of trade, the capacity of the works to do an extended business is now more developed, and your Directors hope next year they may have a more favourable report to present."

Soon after this meeting there came another set-back for poor Edward Phillips. After auditing the accounts, the auditors came to him and revealed that "they had discovered serious defalcations by E. Rowell, the Secretary and Cashier amounting to over £200." Rowell had been entering false amounts of cash-in-hand from time to time, and pocketing the difference. The offence itself was bad enough, £200 was a very large sum to steal, substantially more than the man's annual salary. But the matter was made much worse by the fact of his relationship to the family. He was John Bostock Litherland's brother-in-law, and furthermore his own family was well connected; Lady Burne Jones, Lady Poynter, Rudyard Kipling's mother and Stanley Baldwin's mother were all his first cousins. (91) This had the makings of a major scandal and must be hushed up at all cost.

Edward Phillips would take no action without informing the family, so a Directors' meeting involving only William, Henry and himself was convened. They agreed that Rowell must of course be dismissed but there was no mention of prosecution. William made up the missing sum to the Company out of his own pocket. A week later, on September 7th 1881, a meeting of all the Executive Directors ratified their decision, and Edward Rowell, his wife and two infant children moved out of the old villa in disgrace. In due course he was replaced by another Company Secretary. (92) It appears that the whole episode was successfully kept quiet, but it must have been very distressing for all concerned, and particularly for Edward Phillips. Rowell had been a very important member of the team since his appointment, combining the function of Finance Director and Company Secretary. He had dealt with much of the correspondence of the Company, many of the letters being sent out under his name. It is a terrible thing to find that a close and trusted colleague has been stealing from you.

Nevertheless, after the autumn order-taking season there were signs that at last trade was picking up. Edward Phillips wrote to friends to say that "he was at last able to say that the corner had been turned, that his five anxious years had been rewarded and he looked forward now to more rest and less anxiety in the future." (93)

Then fate struck a terrible and ironic blow. In mid December Phillips was taken ill, and after a few days, on December 15th 1881, he died.

Everyone who worked in the Company must have been shattered; the Company owed almost everything to this one man, its conception, and its nursing into existence and now, just as they all were expecting him to lead them forward into a glorious and profitable future, he was gone.

His executors were his two retailing cousins from London, William and George Phillips, who paid for, (94) and one assumes travelled up to attend his funeral. It took place on 20th December, and he was laid to rest in a simple grave in the old cemetery on the Uttoxeter Road, just a few hundred yards from the house of his friend and supporter, William Bemrose. There will have been a good turn-out for the funeral but mainly from factory people, and the few members of his family who managed to get to Derby. Otherwise his death went relatively unnoticed.

On Boxing Day the remaining Directors met, this time at

59

John McInnes's house in Wallasey on Merseyside, to decide what to do next. First, they moved the following resolution:

"That the Directors cannot adequately express their sense of the loss sustained by them personally and by the Company, through the death of their late colleague Mr. Phillips – as a warm hearted, unselfish, and faithful friend, Mr. Phillips cannot be forgotten by any who had the privilege of his acquaintance. As Managing Director, only the Directors can know the intelligence and assiduity with which he laboured in the establishment of the works, and the subsequent conduct of them, and their regret at his death will be shared by the staff and employees to whom he was ever a kind and considerate master."

Then it was proposed by Mr. Bemrose, seconded by John McInnes "that Henry Litherland and Edward McInnes be appointed Joint Managing Directors."

It is the mark of a good manager that he plans for his own succession, and it was typical of Phillips's thoroughness that even at this early stage in the life of the enterprise he had made sure that his two deputies would be capable of taking the helm. The two boys aged 24 and 30 respectively must have been horrified to be thrust so soon and so unexpectedly into command, but as the shock faded, they must have begun to realise that not only was the worst over, and the ship was steaming ahead into more favourable waters, but that through his training they were well prepared and indeed capable.

These two men, Henry Litherland the senior Managing Director, with commercial responsibility, and Edward McInnes, responsible for production, remained at the helm until August 1924, a period of 42 years. (95)

Only six months later, at the close of that financial year in June, the Directors were able to report to their shareholders that the corner was turned, sales had broken through break-even to nearly £21,000 and the first, if modest, surplus of £230 had been achieved.

What kind of man was Edward Phillips? The first impression of him is that he was a "driven" man. He had been born into a business family, but the business had gone to his cousins so he had to make his own way in the world. Not satisfied with the life of a sales agent he had started his own businesses and in a modest way made a success of them. Still not satisfied, he sold them and put everything he had into Royal Worcester; and after Worcester instead of a comfortable and well deserved retirement, he threw himself headlong into "The Revival of the Derby China Manufacture." As we have seen, obstacle after obstacle presented itself and each one he overcame until the insurmountable final one: his own death.

He cannot have been an easy man; he was not averse to dismissing employees if they were not performing, and he was a terror for refusing to pay bills if he felt that he had not had total satisfaction. (96) He was a perfectionist, a man with a vision and an iron determination to make it a reality, whatever the personal sacrifice. One cannot avoid the suggestion that it was driving himself too hard that caused his early death.

There is very little written about this solitary bachelor; had he survived a few more years to enjoy the success of the Company, he would no doubt have enjoyed some considerable reputation and celebrity. But his personality must have been less than flamboyant to merit an obituary in only one of the four local Derby papers, and only 4 inches in the Pottery Gazette. He had after all spent a lifetime in the industry and served as a Managing Director in two of its great companies.

Yet those who knew him clearly had a great deal of affection for him and he for them. His will, composed only months before his death, with its detailed provisions for annuities for his sisters, and his niece, and including £60 for his faithful housekeeper, Mrs. Everett, reveals a thoughtful and considerate nature. (97) In the words of the obituary in the Derbyshire Advertiser, "as a friend, genial, kind-hearted and generous he will be missed by all those who had the pleasure of his intimate acquaintance. As a master, those who had known him as such showed their feeling and respect at his funeral in a manner most creditable to both. As a son and brother he was amongst the kindest and best. He was

61

also a musician of no mean order and a great lover of the art." Edward Phillips and his colleagues had put an enormous effort and no small amount of money into the creation of this new enterprise. What did it achieve? Was it worth it?

One cannot answer for poor Phillips, who saw only the very beginning of the Company's turn-around into profitability before death removed him from the scene. For those of us who now work in the enterprise, still thriving over a hundred years later, the answer is too obvious. But what of the other founders of the business? They will have looked hard at the fortunes of the business during the decade of the 1880's before congratulating themselves on their wisdom or otherwise.

4. Achieving the Warrant

The years following the death of Edward Phillips saw the blossoming of his creation, and its maturing into one of the world's great china companies.

One of the first matters to be addressed by the Directors was the Art Direction of the Company. Phillips had been his own Art Director, and his unfortunate experience with Richard Binns at Royal Worcester may well have been the reason for his not engaging one. His young successors however, Litherland and McInnes, strongly felt the need to make an appointment and by the following summer they had secured the services of Richard Lunn.

RICHARD LUNN

Lunn had both an academic and a practical background in Art and Design. He had been headmaster at Sheffield School of Art, and before that he had been involved in designing and producing the terracotta decorations for the new buildings at South Kensington and at the Albert Hall. He also had experience in the design of metalwork. (98)

It is clear that his prime interest was in the expensive and artistic end of the business, as, indeed Binns's had been. One cannot imagine Phillips approving of him; the prestigious end of the Company's range of products was important, but profits depended primarily upon filling the factory with commercially attractive merchandise. Despite this, Lunn had a major part to play in the Company's affairs during the 1880's.

His first chance to make his mark came little more than six months after his arrival at the factory, when he was approached

63

by a committee representing the "Liberal working men of Derby" with a proposal which, he must have realised, offered the opportunity of a public relations "coup" of the first order. They wished him to design and manufacture a china service for them to present to the Prime Minister, W. E. Gladstone. (99)

In December 1882 Gladstone had celebrated his political jubilee: 50 years since his entry to public life. As a superb public orator, and a fervent convert to Abraham Lincoln's concept of "government of the people by the people for the people," Gladstone was the hero of the newly enfranchised urban lower middle and working classes. (100) Derby, as a newly industrialised midlands town with a fast-growing working class population, was a typical breeding ground for this hero-worship; this particular group originated from the Midland Railway Company. Gladstone was known as a china collector, and as an admirer of Derby china, so they wished to present him with a service "as a token of their gratitude and esteem."

SAMPLE PLATE FROM THE
GLADSTONE SERVICE

Richard Lunn proposed a 26 piece dessert service of 18 plates, 4 tall and 4 low comports. His senior artist, Count Holtzendorf, was despatched into the countryside to make sketches of local beauty spots which could be converted in hand enamelled scenes on bone china; James Rouse, the celebrated octogenarian china artist who had recently moved from the King Street factory to Osmaston Road, was put in charge of the floral embellishments.

The idea was revealed to the public in the press in April 1883, and in November the committee wrote to the Prime Minister to

JAMES ROUSE

64

invite him to accept the gift at Derby. They received a charming letter in reply accepting the gift, but regretting that he could not manage to come to Derby, from pressure of business, and instead it was arranged that the presentation should be made at Hawarden Castle, his family's country seat near Chester, on Saturday December 22nd.

On the previous Monday, December17th, the service was arranged for display in the Derby Crown Porcelain Company's factory show-room. Invitations were sent to friends and journalists for private viewing on the Monday and Tuesday, and the display was open to the

INVITATION

general public on the Wednesday, Thursday and Friday. It was kept open until late in the evenings, so that the working people could visit after working hours. The Company received a flood of visitors, and there was also a large number of articles in the press complimenting the service, and describing the scene at the factory.

At 7 a.m. on the Great Day, Saturday 22nd, the delegation assembled at Derby Station. It consisted of Alderman Roe, the junior M.P. for Derby, several representatives of the working men, the secretary of the Midland Railway Company, and Richard Lunn bringing with him the precious service, specially packed in a pitch-pine box, and an illuminated address to their hero, framed in oak. They boarded the train for Crewe and changed there for Chester where Mr. Roe entertained them to a large breakfast. They then departed by "brake" for Hawarden, where they were joined by Sir William Harcourt who was not only Gladstone's Home Secretary and close colleague but also the senior M.P. for Derby.

They all assembled in the Library where the service was laid out on the table. Mr. and Mrs. Gladstone, their daughter Helen, and their son Herbert Gladstone M.P. admired the china and the "Grand Old Man" was then addressed formally by Sir William Harcourt, by Mr. Strangeways the working men's secretary, and by Mr. Norman, their chairman. Mr. Gladstone replied with a long speech in which he praised both Derby and Worcester as great china factories which had thrived as free enterprises, unsubsidised by the state as their continental counterparts had been. Then he turned from Free Trade to the further extension of the franchise, ending his speech "...we may go forward... fighting for the masses of our fellow countrymen joining with us in the noble duty which at once invests them with a direct share in all the highest political interests of the country, and the admission of whom...will contribute to the strength and advantage of all portions of the community." He then invited the delegation to luncheon, and afterwards, to an excursion through the Park. (101)

This was, of course, a public relations triumph for the Company, helping to establish it as a major national enterprise. Not all the publicity was entirely favourable to Gladstone, for he was not universally popular. Indeed since the assassination in Dublin the previous year of his close friend and Chief Secretary for Ireland Lord Frederick Cavendish, his personal security had been considerably tightened up in case of an attempt on his own life. The following was not untypical of comment from the Conservative press:

"The Gladstone Service has been on view at the showroom of the Derby 'Crown' Porcelain Company this week. The event has supplied the local sensation of these dull December days. The highest and lowest in the social scale have seen this wonderful example of Art Pottery, the one invited by special card, glowing in the colours of Derby 'Japan', the other made welcome after his working hours. Policemen and Porcelain do not seem to assimilate in sound, but the Derby present in Keramics has been carefully guarded by the Nemesis in blue this week...Hawarden Castle and its approaches are in a sensational state just now. Suppose the sacred box containing the china should be seized as an 'infernal machine' and the deputation treated as conspirators!

"What the cost of the Gladstone Dessert Service has been, the public will never know. The Derby Liberal working men paid the sum of sixty pounds for it. That amount was all they could realise for the great Liberal leader in the most radical borough in the United Kingdom. The rest of the money the Derby 'Crown' Porcelain Company supplied. Multiply sixty pounds by ten and you will nearly approach the sum the Gladstone Service cost producing." (102)

Whatever the truth of this last statement – and £600 was probably a great exaggeration – the loss incurred in helping to fund the working men's present was most certainly money well spent, and achieved an enormous amount of publicity.

Nor did the publicity finish when the delegation returned to Derby, the mission accomplished. Four years later, in October 1887, Gladstone decided to visit Derby and its china factory on his way home to Hawarden from a National Liberal Federation conference at Nottingham. Gladstone had been out of office since the crushing defeat of his attempt to introduce Home Rule for Ireland the previous year, which had split his own party in two. He was still, however, a political superstar, and the newspaper reports describe how at every wayside station between Nottingham and Derby "thousands of persons waved hats and handkerchiefs." They were met by the official party at platform one at 12.30, welcomed and installed in a carriage and pair, decked out in Liberal yellow. Then, preceded by mounted police, followed by the carriages of the welcoming worthies, they drove among cheering crowds up Midland Road and Regent Street to the Derby Crown Works. At the entrance of the factory were Henry Litherland, Edward McInnes and Richard Lunn to greet the Gladstone family and the official party. They were conducted on a tour of the showrooms, and then to the "sending out" room or despatch warehouse where a large number of the workforce were assembled. There was applause and calls for a speech, and of course Gladstone obliged:

"My friends" he said "I have had the greatest pleasure of

seeing your works. I am only sorry that the limit as to time prevents me from doing more than expressing that pleasure in the briefest terms. The progress of this great manufacture is to me a matter of great interest, not only from a national point of view; because I have always had a very great love for the fine art of production of porcelain, and a very particular interest in those great schools of porcelain which have advanced the history of England. I heartily wish you, and the great works you are connected with, prosperity and advancement in a very remarkable branch of art."

The two young Managing Directors, Litherland and McInnes, then presented Mrs. Gladstone with a little cup and saucer of white porcelain with gilt decoration in a case, and the party then remounted the carriages and drove away, to the applause of the crowds. (103)

Alas, none of these important events were enjoyed by William Litherland, the other original partner with Edward Phillips. Only months before the completion of the Gladstone Service, in April 1883, he died at his home in Laurel Road, Fairfield, Liverpool, aged 80 years. As one of his obituaries recalled "he was one of the oldest, best known and most respected of the shop-keeping class of this city." (104) In addition to that, he enjoyed the distinction, along with his partner Phillips, not only of having saved the Worcester factory from extinction and brought it to a state of healthy profitability, but also of having, in their own words "Revived the Art of China Manufacture in Derby." It was tragic that neither of these two ceramic heroes saw the full fruition of their efforts at Derby.

William Litherland was succeeded as Chairman by John McInnes, the third of the original partners and founders of the Company. But McInnes senior was an old and sick man, and although he visited the factory occasionally and enjoyed himself in visiting the laboratory, encouraging the factory chemist, Tom Hough, in his experiments with bodies, glazes and colours, he remained most of the time at his home at Wallasey. Most of the board meetings which he chaired were held there, and most of the remainder, which took place in Derby, were chaired by William Bemrose acting as his deputy. Despite his infirmity, however, he remained Chairman of the Company until his death in 1897.

Throughout the 1880's, The Derby Crown Porcelain Company gradually gained in reputation and prestige. Just as in the 18th century, and indeed in the 20th, Royal patronage was the ultimate accolade. In 1886 came the first evidence that the Queen herself approved of the Company's efforts. A certain Mr. Jenkins organised an exhibition of modern ceramics in Edinburgh, which Queen Victoria visited. As the newspaper reported, the "Crown Derby China...is a notable collection, consisting for the most part of specimens of the Old Derby blue and gold. Her Majesty the Queen, after admiring the Derby pieces, ordered some fine specimens from the Derby factory of the mottled blue and gold just introduced by the Derby Crown Porcelain Company, with a success that has excited the interest of the ceramic world." (105)

It was therefore not surprising that when it was reported that the Ladies of Worcester proposed to send some Royal Worcester Porcelain as a present to Her Majesty for her Jubilee in 1887, an article appeared in the local papers urging the Ladies of Derby to follow suit. Naturally, the good ladies took up the challenge.

Under the leadership of the Mayoress of Derby a committee was formed in April 1887, Mr. Lunn was once again asked to design a suitable offering, and subscriptions, maximum one guinea, were invited from "the wives and daughters of our leading citizens."

As it happened, Mr. Lunn had already begun work on a presentation. In January, the Directors had asked him to prepare a gift for the Queen (106) but they must have realised that for reasons of protocol she might well refuse to accept it, since it was offered directly by a commercial concern. The approach from the ladies' committee provided a better means of ensuring that the gift reached Her Majesty; it also enabled the presentation to be ready quite remarkably quickly by July, when the Jubilee celebrations were at their height.

The gift consisted of two 20" tall vases with crown lids, and a plaque. All three items were richly decorated with plenty of mazarine blue and gold, and a scheme of design packed with every kind of symbolism, from the Muses to Imperial Heraldry.

The items carried suitable inscriptions, the rim of the plaque even containing a quotation from a speech of the late Prince Albert, concerning man's Divine Purpose. The overall design was by Lunn, the enamelling was by J. L. Chapman, and the raised paste gilding by Thomas Brown with help from William Piper. Subscribers were invited to send donations to Messrs. Bemrose or to the offices of the Derbyshire Advertiser. The palace was consulted about the propriety of the gift and a letter was received from Sir Henry Ponsonby stating that it would indeed be welcome and give Her Majesty great pleasure.

THE ANNOUNCEMENT OF
THE QUEEN'S JUBILEE GIFT

During the week of July 15th the present was on show in the factory showroom, and it was then sent for display at the City Art Gallery for two days. The items were boxed in mahogany cases lined in crimson plush, and accompanied by an illuminated address from the ladies, on vellum and bound in red morocco, produced by Messrs. Bemrose. The gift was then despatched to Balmoral. (107)

There is no doubt that all these exotic presentations represented the tip of an iceberg of "succes d'estime." But what of financial success?

We must look at the financial performance of the Derby Crown Porcelain Company in the context of the general economic climate of 19th century Britain. It is certain that the timing of the founders could have been happier, since the last quarter of the century was a great deal more difficult for the capitalist than its middle years; indeed Phillips and Litherland might have done better to have ignored Worcester, and gone straight to Derby in 1862.

Britain had been the first country to harness the power of the new technology of the Industrial Revolution to the rapidly growing population, coming into the towns from the countryside, and breeding at an unprecedented rate. While the rest of Europe was caught up with revolution and political instability, Britain was exploiting its colonial and imperial markets, and enjoying an unprecedented boom. The boom, however began to fade in the 1880's.

Not only were other nations beginning to catch up and provide fierce competition, but many of them began increasingly to favour protectionist tariffs against foreign imports. British businessmen and politicians for whom Free Trade had been an article of faith, began instead to talk about Fair Trade. In particular the Americans imposed heavy tariffs on imported goods, which were greatly increased in the 1890's by the McInley tariff, and which dealt Royal Crown Derby a very severe if temporary blow. (108)

THE DERBY CROWN PORCELAIN COMPANY: FINANCIAL PERFORMANCE 1877/90

Financial Year	Sales	Profit (Loss)	Dividends: 6% Preference £10,500 (at par)		Ordinaries £37,350 (83 at £450)	
	£	£	%	£	%	£
77/8	755	(?)	–	–	–	–
78/9	6,080	(?)	–	–	–	–
79/80	14,530	(?)	–	–	–	–
80/81	15,720	(?)	–	–	–	–
81/82	20,720	230	–	–	–	–
82/83	22,820	1,743	6%	630	2½%	933
83/84	24,854	2,834	6%	630	5%	1867
84/85	25,253	3,111	6%	630	5%	1867
85/86	20,284	2,000	6%	630	5%	1867
86/87	21,806	1,404	6%	630	2½%	933
87/88	19,918	664	6%	630	–	–
88/89	20,246	950	6%	630	1%	373
89/90	24,746	1,994	6%	630	2½%	933
1880/90 TOTAL DIVIDENDS				5,040		8,773
% RETURN FOR DECADE			(48%)		(23½%)	

NOTES:

1) Average return on sales 1881 – 90: 7.4%

2) Average % yield: on preference shares 1880/90 4.8% on ordinary shares 1880/90: 2.3% See footnote (113)

The Company's internal teething difficulties, as we have seen, were overcome in the year of Edward Phillips's death, 1881, and the Company had a splendid run of sales and profits for four years until 1887, the year of the jubilee and of Gladstone's visit. In 1884/5 the ratio of profits to sales reached an enviable 12%, and ordinary shareholders received a 5% dividend, which in an era of zero inflation was a very satisfactory return. Things were going so well that the Directors considered their showrooms in Ely Place too small and took larger premises at 42 Holborn Viaduct. The two young Managing Directors' salaries were increased from £200 to £300 in 1883, and from £300 to £500 in 1884. By the mid '80's the workforce had reached around 400, and the weekly wage bill reached nearly £290. A new warehouse and polishing shop was constructed, and £2,000 of 5% debentures stock originally taken by John McInnes was repaid. (109)

However, after 1887 trade became much more difficult, sales fell back perilously close to the break-even level, and for the financial year 1887/8 the ordinary shareholders received no dividend. Inevitably, stresses and strains inside the Company revealed themselves. In August 1888 the Directors met at John McInnes's house at Wallasey. They decided that with trade in its present state it was time to make a change in the Art Direction of the company. "Mr. Lunn was not a suitable man for his post, his tastes and talents being chiefly in the getting up of expensive articles which were exceedingly difficult to dispose of." They decided to give him notice and to advertise for a new designer. One has to suspect that behind this short board minute, there lay something of a re-run of the saga of Binns and Phillips at Worcester, years before; the potential for conflict between the temperamental Art Director and the practical Pottery Manager is so often present. Lunn was not the only casualty: Mr. Lea, foreman of potters since the early years was dismissed "as he did not attend properly to his duties."

But in spite of these difficulties, the Company's performance over the decade was respectable. The average return on sales at 7.4% is more or less what one would expect from a modern business, taking bad years with good. With zero inflation, the return for preference shareholders was good by modern standards, that for ordinary shareholders not bad, but erratic.

In order to measure the success of the founders of the Derby Crown Porcelain Company one must look back at the original objectives of the enterprise.

Their first objective, or in modern business studies jargon, their Mission, was encapsulated in the title of their first share prospectus "The Revival of the Derby China Manufacture" (see appendix III). Time and time again this phrase, or variations of it, appear in board minutes, and in newspaper articles. Despite poor Sampson Hancock's protest that Derby china had never died, it was this Great Idea which motivated them, and which without doubt they achieved. By building on the traditions of the past, they established a fine, if modest sized business with the highest standards of craftsmanship, technical skill and design, and an international reputation.

A secondary objective was to develop a substantial share of both home and export markets, particularly North America. In this too they succeeded, particularly in the USA which from the first year of operations provided an enthusiastic source of business for the Company, and this in spite of excessively high tariffs. As one journalist wrote:

"A dinner service for the American market gives us pause. The Americans are the largest purchasers from the Derby Works. They take the most costly of the productions...what do you think of a dinner service for £200?...Add to this original cost 50% duty at the exorbitantly exacting custom house at New York, then add another 50% for the American dealers' profit. This sum...makes the dinner crockery of the wealthy American come to something like a cool £400. But it is a magnificent show he puts upon his table." (110)

A third objective was the construction of a modern, clean, spacious and elegant factory, with housing for the workforce, in pleasant green surroundings, a pleasure to work in and to visit. Certainly in the opinion of visiting journalists they succeeded in this. One example, writing for the Preston Guardian in 1883, described the works as follows:

"I have visited this factory frequently...and from my by no means small experience of factories and workshops, I can safely assert that in few there is greater comfort or a happier set of men, women, boys and girls. Wages are good, overtime is not rare, and above all the workpeople seem proud of their calling and interested in all they are doing." (111)

The underlying objective of course was to provide a good

return on capital, and in this as we have seen they were modestly successful.

The ultimate and literally, crowning measure of success, however, came in January 1890. In late 1889 one of the Aldermen of Derby, Mr. Hobson, suggested to the Directors that it was now appropriate that the Company, like that in Worcester, should be granted permission to use the title Royal, and indeed, the Royal Warrant with the privilege to use the Royal Arms. He undertook to forward a statement by the Company in support of its prayer for these privileges, to the Duke of Devonshire, who was Lord Lieutenant of the county and Lord High Steward of Derby.

The statement was a lengthy document outlining the history of Derby China from the 18th century, in particular mentioning the various Royal commissions over the years, and describing the modern company: "The present works...have been established over twelve years with a capital of £65,850 and are in a prosperous condition employing about 280 hands." It pointed out the benefits of prestige and position these privileges would bestow, particularly in important export markets, and quoted widely from Mr. Gladstone's speech praising the Company on the occasion of the presentation at Harwarden Castle.

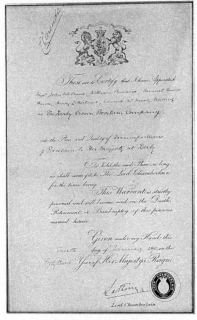

THE ROYAL WARRANT

Alderman Hobson soon received a reply from the Marquess of Hartington advising the Directors to write to the Secretary of State for Home Affairs. This they did, on 24th December 1889 and on 3rd January 1890 they received a reply from a Home Office official.

"I am directed by the Secretary of State to acquaint you that he has had the honour to lay your application before the Queen, and that Her Majesty has been graciously pleased to accede to your request and to command that the Derby Crown Porcelain Company be called the Royal Crown Derby Porcelain Company." (112)

And that, barring the completion of legalities, was the glorious end of the Derby Crown Porcelain Company, and the auspicious beginning of Royal Crown Derby.

Conclusion

*T*he story of the founding and development of this Victorian manufacturing business, the Derby Crown Porcelain Company, is remarkable as a chronicle of human endeavour and determination, beset by difficulties, but finally crowned by success.

In particular, the character of Edward Phillips emerges as the dominant and driving force behind the enterprise, and it seems extraordinary that so little is known about him. As managing director of Royal Worcester he pulled that company from losses into profit, and enabled Richard Binns to re-establish its leading position in the world of ceramic art. As founder and Managing Director at Derby he created from scratch a rival business of the first order almost single handedly. These achievements should have established him as one of the leading lights of a great British industry. And yet, little is known about him, almost nothing has been written about him, we do not even have a portrait of him.

However the story is also remarkable because it contains so many elements which connect it to the universal themes of 19th century history and of the modern business world which emerged from it. The migration of labour to the towns, the harnessing of that labour to capital and new technology, the rising prosperity of the middle class, the growth of municipal pride and ambition, and of town planning and development, the extension of the franchise, the impact of the economic growth of North America; all these themes and more are exemplified in this story.

Furthermore, the student of business will recognise many familiar themes too.

All the problems of business start-ups are here in full; the unpredictability of new businesses and the need to react quickly and flexibly to changing events, the problems of financing, and of achieving a balance of reward between original capital and new capital, the importance of a management team utterly committed to its mission, the fact that success, if it comes at all, comes more slowly and expensively than anyone would have dared to suggest; all these will be instantly recognisable to the modern venture capitalist.

It is this multi faceted interest which has encouraged me to take this story into print, and to provide a modest monument to the memory of all those individuals, named and unnamed, who created the Derby Crown Porcelain Company, and laid the foundations of a famous and excellent business, Royal Crown Derby.

Footnotes

Source:
1) Llewellynn Jewitt – *Ceramic Art of Great Britain*, J.S.Virtue & Co 1883/4: see Phillips & Bagster.
2) Geoffrey Godden – *Encyclopaedia of British Pottery and Porcelain Marks*, Herbert Jenkins 1964.
3) Derbyshire County Records Office:. E. Phillips's will.
4) Royal Crown Derby Archive: Edward McInnes's Factory Cuttings Book page 9.
5) Ibid: page 14.
6) Letter from Litherland's descendant the late Mr. Angus Bell to his cousin Mr. John Yolland – Royal Crown Derby Archive.
7) Royal Crown Derby Archive: Edward McInnes's Factory Cuttings Book page 14.
8) Henry Sandon – *Royal Worcester Porcelain from 1862 to the Present Day*, Barrie & Jenkins 1989.
9) Royal Crown Derby Archive: Factory Cuttings Book page 9.
10) Royal Worcester's Company Minute Book.
11) Royal Crown Derby Archive: Title of the Prospectus for shares in Derby Crown Porcelain Company 1877.
12) Marilyn Swain – William Bemrose; Derby Porcelain International Society Journal I, 1988.
13) Liverpool Daily Post December 10th 1896.
14) J.Twitchett – *Royal Crown Derby*, Antique Collectors' Club 1988: page66 describes McInnes working in the factory with Thomas Hough, works chemist.
15) Royal Crown Derby Archive: First factory accounts journal; shows rent shared between H. Litherland and E. McInnes for 100 Osmaston Road.
16) Ibid: Factory Cuttings Book. Barrow News November 28th 1885 – Report of Henry Litherland's wedding at St. Clement Danes, London. Also lists Warrington Hogg as a wedding guest.
17) Contemporary accounts include Pottery Gazette October 1st 1880, Derbyshire Advertiser April 14th 1881, British Mail December 1881 – all in E.McInnes's cuttings book as above.
18) Royal Crown Derby Archive: envelope 1.
19) Ibid: envelope 11.
20) Ibid: Derby Crown Porcelain Company prospectus spring 1877.
21) 1852 Map of Litchurch, Derby Local Studies Library.
22) Royal Crown Derby Archive.
23) Ibid: envelope 4.
24) Derbyshire Advertiser October 29th 1875: Report of proceedings of Derby Board of Guardians.

25) Derby Census, Osmaston Road 1881.
26) Derby Advertiser and Derby Reporter November 17th 1875: letter to the editors.
27) Derbyshire Advertiser February 17th 1876: letter to the editor.
28) Derby Mercury March 24th 1876.
29) Royal Crown Derby Archive: Factory Newspaper Cuttings Book page 37. Preston Guardian December 22nd 1883 – "the Art Directorship, which Mr. Phillips had undertaken, passed to Mr. Richard Lunn."
30) Royal Crown Derby Archive: Factory Newspaper Cuttings Book page 66.
31) *"The House of Bemrose"* published 1926. Also Royal Crown Derby Archive: Factory Newspaper Cuttings Book page 46. Sheffield Telegraph September 1884, also page 50 Sheffield Telegraph September 1886, also page 65.
32) Royal Crown Derby Archive: envelope 13.
33) Ibid: envelope 13.
34) Ibid: envelope 13.
35) Local Studies Library, Derby.
36) Royal Crown Derby Archive: Factory Cuttings Book newspaper article page 66.
37) Kelly's Directory of Derbyshire 1895.
38) Royal Crown Derby Minute Book May 23rd 1887.
39) A Century of Trade 1876-1976, published by the Department of Trade and Industry for the centenary of the Patent Office, chapter 2.
40) Royal Crown Derby Archive: envelope 11.
41) Ibid: envelope 11.
42) Ibid: Sampson Hancock papers.
43) Royal Crown Derby Archive: Sales Journal 1878.
44) Derby Porcelain International Society newsletter no. 17: J.Twitchett; story of Old Crown Derby China.
45) Evidence concerning the factory's construction, layout and operation comes from Royal Crown Derby Archive, quotations, correspondence etc., in envelopes 3,4,5,7 and 12, also contemporary descriptions of the works in newspaper articles in the Factory Cuttings Book. Also, importantly from Mr. Joe Crossley, retired sliphouse foreman (among other jobs) who joined the factory in the late 20's before it was radically altered by the Robinson family.
46) *Royal Crown Derby* by Twitchett & Bailey – Antique Collectors' Club 1988: 3rd Edition page 66.
47) Royal Crown Derby Archive: Factory Cuttings Book page 6 – British Mail December 1881.
48) Ibid: envelope 12.
49) Joe Crossley.
50) Royal Crown Derby Archive: Eddowes's bill.
51) Ibid: Factory Cuttings Book page 66.
52) Ibid: page 6.
53) Ibid: envelope 12.

54) Ibid: Factory Cuttings Book page 66.
55) 1881 Census – 102 Osmaston Road. Also Edward Phillips's will left Mrs. Everett £50.
56) Royal Crown Derby Archive: envelope 7.
57) Ibid: Factory Cuttings Book page 66.
58) Minton Archive.
59) Royal Crown Derby Archive: Accounts Journal.
60) Twitchett & Bailey op.cit page 59.
61) Royal Crown Derby Archive.
62) Ibid: envelope 13, letter Landgraf to W. Litherland
63) Ibid: Factory Cuttings Book, several articles.
64) Twitchett op.cit. page 242.
65) Royal Crown Derby Minute Book.
66) Family tree in the papers of the late Mr. Angus Bell, Litherland descendant – Royal Crown Derby Archive.
67) Royal Crown Derby Minute Book.
68) Ibid.
69) See Baker: "Potworks", Royal Commission on historical monuments 1991.
70) Royal Crown Derby Archive: envelope 7, Hewitt & Alexander correspondence.
71) Royal Crown Derby Minute Book.
72) See footnote 52.
73) Royal Crown Derby Accounts Journal and 1881 Census.
74) Royal Crown Derby Minute Book
75) Royal Crown Derby Accounts Journal.
76) Royal Crown Derby Minute Book July 1909.
77) Royal Crown Derby Archive: envelope 1.
78) See Baker op.cit.
79) Royal Crown Derby Archive: envelope 1.
80) See footnote 16.
81) Royal Crown Derby Archive: envelope 3.
82) Ibid: Factory Cuttings Book page 4.
83) Ibid: envelope 3
84) Royal Crown Derby Minute Book.
85) Royal Crown Derby Archive: envelope 3.
86) Ibid: Sales Journal.
87) McInnes family bible confirms date of birth 1859 as told to J.Twitchett by a family member in 1977.
88) 1881 Census, and obituary in factory cuttings book.
89) Factory Minute Book.
90) Ibid.
91) Family tree in the papers of the late Mr. Angus Bell, Litherland's descendant – Royal Crown Derby Archive.
92) Factory Minute Book.

93) Royal Crown Derby Archive: Factory Cuttings Book, obituary of E. Phillips page 9.
94) Director of Cemeteries, Derby.
95) Royal Crown Derby Archive: Factory Cuttings Book page 81.
96) Apart from those disputes already mentioned there was an argument with Jones, the timber merchant, and with Jenks and Holt, suppliers of showcases damaged in transit – Royal Crown Derby Archive: envelope 11.
97) Edward Phillips's will. His estate was eventually valued at, £6,600.
98) Royal Crown Derby Archive: Factory Cuttings Book pages 30, 37,38.
99) The account of the events surrounding the presentation of the Gladstone Service are taken from numerous cuttings in the Factory Cuttings Book pages 13-44.
100) See *Gladstone, A Biography* by Phillip Magnus, Murray 1954.
101) Royal Crown Derby Archive: Factory Cuttings Book pages 22-44.
102) Ibid: page 30.
103) Royal Crown Derby Archive: Factory Cuttings Book pages56-58.
104) Ibid: page 14.
105) Ibid: page 50.
106) Company Minute Book.
107) Royal Crown Derby Archive: Factory Cuttings Book pages 51-55.
108) Donald Read: *England 1868-1914*, Longman 1979.
109) Company Minute Book
110) Royal Crown Derby Archive: Factory Cuttings Book page.20.
111) Ibid: page 37.
112) Company Minute Book
113) Since no complete accounts for the Company have survived, these figures have been arrived at as follows:
1) The profit or surplus each year appears in the Minute Book starting at 1881/2.
2) Sales for the first years have been calculated by totting up the monthly sales totals in the first (and only) Sales Journal.
3) Sales in subsequent years are calculated using (2) as a base, but adding or subtracting the sum by which the minutes of the AGM's report sales as having increased or decreased.
4) Both the % and £ dividend values are reported in the Minute Book.
Although the prospectus for the preference shares states that in years when there is insufficient profit to pay the interest the arrears will be carried forward, no arrears were paid for the years before the first dividend in 1882/3.

Appendix I

Edward Phillips – Background

*I*n the Factory Cuttings Book in the Archive at Royal Crown Derby there is an obituary of Edward Phillips marked "Derbyshire Advertiser, December 1881"

According to this he "was born in Harley Street and in early life became identified with the earthenware and porcelain trade."

Harley Street seems far too grand an address for Phillips: there was certainly no Phillips in the 1841 Census living there – the inhabitants were mostly gentry and nobility. Were his parents domestics? Or was he born in the Harley Street area? Anyway, he was a Londoner.

"He commenced his business career as the representative of Messrs. Chas. Mee & Sons (now Old Hall Earthenware) jointly with Messrs. Tho. Webb & Sons...Mr. Phillips afterwards became an enamel colour maker...after some years of travelling...he settled at Hanley and commenced to decorate white china...and also the manufacture of glass."

According to Geoffrey Godden "Edward potted (or rather decorated) at Shelton, Hanley c.1855-62."

According to the obituary, in 1862 he sold up and went to Worcester, and came to Derby in 1876. In 1881 "he was somewhat suddenly called to rest in his 65th year."

So he was born in 1816.

The Pottery Gazette of February 1st 1882 published another short obituary. According to this "he was interred in the Old Cemetery, Derby" and "in early life this gentleman represented, in the country, the firm of Guest Wood & Guest, glass manufacturers of Dudley." No mention of Old Hall, nor Webb – is there a connection between the latter and Guest, Wood & Guest? Or was this the glass mentioned later, in the first obituary or perhaps he sold it alongside his own china? Or perhaps this was a completely separate job.

However, the Director of Cemeteries in Derby tells us that Edward Phillips occupies grave number 3,002 in the old Uttoxeter Road cemetery and this was paid for by William Philip Phillips of 155 New Bond Street, London.

We also find that in October 1882 at a Derby Crown Porcelain Company board meeting, "the offer by Messrs. W. P. & G. Phillips of the shares held by the late Mr. E. Phillips was placed before the meeting" (the shares were eventually bought by Phillips's founding partners, John McInnes and William Litherland).

So W. P. & G. Phillips were clearly his executors, but what relation to him were they? Edward Phillips's will appoints "my cousins William Philip Phillips and George Phillips, carrying on business at 359 Oxford Street and 155 New Bond Street London to be my executors..." Other relations mentioned in the will are "...my sisters Mary Jane Phillips and Elizabeth Owen Phillips... Fanny Phillips, the adopted daughter of my sister Mary Jane... my brother Jonathan Phillips now residing in Canada."

He had no direct heirs, and he lived on his own with a housekeeper in Derby. It seems likely that he was a bachelor and that W. P. & G. Phillips were first cousins.

W.P. & G. Phillips were china and glass retailers in London, and were important customers from the first month of Derby Crown sales records, with orders both for Oxford Street and for Bond Street.

In the Minton Museum there is a desk set in the centre of which is the following inscription: "Presented by H. Minton to his friend George Phillips on his first visit to the Staffs. Potteries November 25th, 1848." (See illustration in The Dictionary of Minton by Paul Atterbury page 127.)

According to Geoffrey Godden's Encyclopedia of Marks W. P. & G. Philips operated at 358 and 359 Oxford Street from 1858-97. According to Kelly's Directory of 1841 there was a Jonathan Phillips described as "chinaman" at the same address – also described as "china, glass and earthenware dealers." Was Jonathan W. P. & G.'s father and Edward's uncle? Or vice-versa?

Again and going back another generation according to Geoffrey Godden, a partnership of George Phillips and John Martin in Oxford Street ended in 1789, and George Phillips then carried on alone, and supplied Duesbury with goods in September 1793 from 133 Oxford Street. In November 1813 J. & J. Phillips, chinamen of 359 Oxford Street announced to "the nobility gentry and the public, that the business would in future be carried on by them on the same premise." So presumably J. and J. were George's sons and/or heirs.

If Jonathan was one J., who was the other?

According to Jewitt, the Church Works in Hanley, which had belonged to Wilson and Neale earthenware manufacturers in the early 1800's, was rented by Jacob Phillips and by his partner John Denton Bagster." According to Pat Halfpenny at Stoke City Museum, Mr. Bagster's gravestone says he was a Londoner. In Jewitt's words "the Phillips of this firm was Jacob, brother to Jonathan Phillips of Oxford Street London, and uncle to the present Messrs. Phillips of Oxford Street."

So surely Jacob was the other J., come up from London with Bagster to secure supplies for his and his brother's London retail business.

It seems coincidental that Edward also came up to Stoke to manufacture in Shelton – like father like son? Perhaps.

Going back further into the 18th and 17th centuries Richard Kilburn has traced a series of china and/or glass dealers called Phillips, starting with George, founder of the glass seller's company in 1664, who died in 1675. He was also a wholesaler of London Delftware and Dwight's stoneware.

There was a Samuel and a James who became freemen of the company in 1677 and 1723.

In 1750-1 there was a John who sold Bow China to Lord Egremont at Petworth. He dealt from Swallow Street and bought earthenware from John Wedgwood in 1763.

In 1774 a John, chinaman of Crown Street, St.James, was imprisoned for debt.

In 1792 a Phillips and Finch were listed as glass sellers in Berkeley Square.

It seems likely that at least some of these Phillipses were from the same family, and possible that our Edward was a member of it. Unfortunately Phillips is a very common name, and so far we have no proof of any exact relationships.

Appendix II

Comparative Wages and Prices: 1880's to 1990's

1880 SALARIES

NAME	POSITION	REMUNERATION	PER ANNUM	DATE
E. Phillips (1)	Managing Director	£500 (+ exp) p.a.	£500	1877
H. Litherland ⎱		£200 p.a.	£200	1881-3
Ed. McInnes ⎰ Joint M.D's		then £300 p.a.	£300	1883-4
		then £400 p.a.	£400	1884
E. Rowell	Company Secretary	£ 10 p.m.	£120	1880
A. H. Bowles	Company Secretary	£ 20 p.m.	£240	1885
W. Pepper	Company Secretary	£120 p.a.	£120	1893
Richard Lunn	Art Director	£ 88/15/-p.q.	£355	1882
T. Reed	Art Director	£ 25 p.m.	£300	1889
W. Hogg	Assistant Art Dir. & Head Modeller	£225 p.a.	£225	1889
W. R. Ingram	Head Modeller	£300 p.a.	£300	1876
Will. Stephan	Modeller	£ 3/3/- p.w.	£156/8s.	1876
Desire Leroy	Senior Artist	£225 p.a.	£225	1890
Landgraf	Senior Artist	£ 25 p.m.	£300	1878
Holtzendorf (2)	Senior Artist	£ 7 p.m.	£ 84	1878
G. W. Darlington	Artist	£ 2 p.w.	£104	1897
A. H. Folker	Senior Salesman & London Manager	£400 p.a.	£400	1894
C. N. Owen	Senior Salesman	£ 45 p.q.	£180	1888
S. H. Owen	Junior Salesman	£ 6 p.m.	£ 72	1888
Newlands	Country Sales Rep.	£ 12/10/- p.w.	£650	1880
Spiers	London Manager	£ 12/10/- p.w.	£650	1880
A. Heath	Foreman of Potters	£ 2/5/- p.w.	£117	1889
A. Heath	Clerk (before promotion above)	£ 1/18/- p.w.	£ 98/8s.	1888
W. Pepper	Clerk (before promotion above)	£ 1/8/- p.w.	£ 72/8s.	1888
Parkinson	Junior Clerk	12/- p.w.	£ 31/2s.	1888
Collier	Junior Clerk (replaced Parkinson)	18/- p.w.	£ 46/8s.	1888

NOTES:

1) At Worcester, Phillips, as Joint Managing Director had received £600 plus bonus.

2) Holtzendorf must have been paid a retainer of £7, or else was contracted to do less work than Landgraf.

General: These details are taken from the Minute Books, the Cash Books or from contracts (Royal Crown Derby Archive: envelope 13). We know the labour force fluctuated between about 300 and 400 in the Derby Crown period. The weekly wages sum which appears in the Cash Books ranges from £190 to about £290. Piece-work and overtime would distort the relationship between the total wages bill and the number employed, but ignoring this, the average wage would be 12/5d to 13/-.

MODERN SALARY AND WAGE LEVELS

The following annual salary or wage levels represent those one would have to consider offering if one was setting up a china business of 300/400 employees in the Midlands in 1991.

1)	Managing Director of quality pottery factory employing 300	£50,000
2)	Company Secretary	£25,000
3)	Art Director	£25,000
4)	Head Modeller	£18,000
5)	Modeller	£12,000
6)	Senior hand enameller or specialist gilder	£10,400
7)	London Manager	£25,000
8)	Area Sales Representative	£15,000
9)	Production Manager	£15,000
10)	Accounts Clerk Senior	£8,000
11)	Accounts Clerk Junior	£6,000

PRICE RISES 1900 – 1990

	1900 £	1990 £	Factor
Railway. London/Glasgow			
2nd class return	1.66	59.00	36
Atlantic crossing – ship cheapest	12.33	970.00	79
Bottle of whisky	0.18	8.80	49
Dinner at Savoy	0.38	28.75	76
Opera ticket Covent Garden: cheapest	0.13	3.00	23
Opera ticket Covent Garden: dearest	1.50	101.00	67
Coal (household) ton	1.18	121.00	102
Economist Magazine	0.03	1.60	93
Ticket at Theatre Royal: cheapest	0.06	7.50	125
Ticket at Theatre Royal: most expensive	0.60	25. 00	42
Gold oz.	4.24	209.16	49
Undergraduate fee, London University	48.88	1675.00	34
Mens handmade shoes	0.84	125.00	149
Dunhill pipe	0.38	108.00	284
Taxi fare – 1 mile	0.03	1.60	53
Lighter, gold plated	1.75	185.00	106
Potatoes (7lbs)	0.02	0.91	46

	Pence	Pence	
Loaf of bread	0.5	0.42	84
Milk (pint)	0.7	0.30	43
Stamp London/Scotland	0.42	0.22	52
Times Newspaper	0.83	0.35	42
Underground ticket	0.83	0.70	84
		Average.	78

Source: *Economist Magazine*, December 22nd 1990, page 128.

Appendix III

REVIVAL OF THE DERBY CHINA MANUFACTURE.

PROVISIONAL PROSPECTUS.

The Derby Crown Porcelain Company,

LIMITED.

Capital £80,000 in 160 Shares of £500 each.

£20 PER SHARE ON APPLICATION, £80 PER SHARE ON ALLOTMENT,
AND £50 THREE MONTHS AFTER ALLOTMENT.

The balance to be called up as and when required by the Directors. It is expected that 75 per cent. is the utmost that will ι called up.

Directors.

MR. WILLIAM BEMROSE, OF ELMHURST, LONSDALE PLACE, DERBY, IN THE COUNTY OF DERBY, PUBLISHER.

MR. WILLIAM LITHERLAND, OF LAUREL ROAD, LIVERPOOL, IN THE COUNTY OF LANCASTER, GLASS AND CHINA DEALER.

MR. EDWARD PHILLIPS, OF LADY GROVE, LITCHURCH, IN THE COUNTY OF DERBY, CHINA MANUFACTURER.

Bankers.

MESSRS. W. & S. EVANS & Co., DERBY.

Solicitor.

MR. C. K. EDDOWES, DERBY.

Architect.

MR. E. L. MADDOCK, HANLEY.

Secretary (pro tem).

MR. C. K. EDDOWES.

Temporary Offices.

No. 4, ALBERT STREET, DERBY.

89

THIS Company is formed for the purpose of re-establishing the manufacture of Porcelain and Opaque Crown China, for which Derby was formerly so celebrated.

It is intended to produce a manufacture of a quality which shall take rank with the first houses in the trade for perfection of composition and high artistic finish.

The Works are situated in the Osmaston Road, Derby, and have been commenced from plans by and under the supervision of Mr. Edward Phillips, who has had a long experience in the business, and was one of the Partners who took over the Worcester Works from the unsuccessful hands of private individuals, and was mainly instrumental in the last ten years in securing for it the commercial success which it now enjoys.

In June, 1875, about an acre-and-half of building land, adjoining the Derby Workhouse, was bought for £2,500; on this ground, a mill has been erected, with slip houses and other buildings; and machinery, and a fifty-horse engine are being fixed, which, with the buildings, will cost over £7,000.

In December last, the adjoining site of the Derby Union Workhouse, with 13,400 yards of land, and all the buildings, boundary walls, &c., was bought for £9,150.

This must be regarded as a most advantageous purchase, as the buildings are in good order, and will, with a moderate expenditure, be made available for t purpose of the Company, and are capable of giving accommodation for the emp¹ ment of nearly one thousand hands.

Ovens and kilns are now being erected on a portion of this land in accordance with a plan to combine the two properties, and if full possession of the buildings and other parts of the site can (as promised), be obtained early in the summer, it is hoped that with reasonable progress on the part of the building contractor, the business of the Company may be commenced in the autumn of the present year.

The services of a gentleman of high class reputation as a Sculptor and Modeller have been secured as head Modeller; other Modellers and Mould Makers have also been for some months at work in premises rented for workshops.

Plans are ready, and it is intended at once to commence building twenty residences on the Company's land, for the Manager, Artists, and other principal Emp oyés. The area of the first land purchased which is not built upon, and will not be required for the works, will be ample for the purpose.

The front of the present Workhouse buildings will be rebuilt and converted into a handsome elevation, containing extensive Show Rooms, open to visitors, and the open space in front will be laid out ornamentally with a spacious carriage approach to the front entrance.

3

It was at first intended that this undertaking should be commenced and carried on as a private partnership, consisting of three partners, Mr. PHILLIPS, before mentioned, Mr. LITHERLAND, of Liverpool, and Mr. McINNES, of Wallasey, near Birkenhead, but at the desire of one of the partners, who does not wish to withdraw any portion of his share, but for family reasons desires to limit his liability, it has been determined to register it as a Limited Company, with a small number of proprietors.

The total capital will be £80,000, divided into 160 Shares of £500 each. But it is thought that it will be necessary to call up only three-fourths of this sum by instalments, and to raise what, if any, may be further required by mortgage and debenture. The articles will provide that any Shareholder desiring to dispose of his Shares shall give the option of purchase (of course, on equality of conditions), to a Director or existing Shareholder in the Company.

Of the 160 Shares, 80 will be applied for by the persons at present interested, and 5 Shares are proposed to be reserved for Employés, leaving 75 Shares, which it is proposed to offer to gentlemen connected with the County of Derby, who may desire to promote the success of a manufacture for which the county has been so famed.

All the capital called up will be paid in cash, and no promotion money, premiums, commissions, or any such allowance will be made to any one. The capital account will be charged with the cost price of the land as purchased, with interest thereon until the commencement of the working, and with an allowance to Mr. Phillips from the date of his active employment in June, 1875, of £500 a year as salary, and £100 a year for travelling expenses, and these together with the cost of building, machinery, wages to Modellers, Mould Makers, and others, and cost of materials, carriage, &c., will form the items of the Capital account.

A Mortgage of £10,000 has been arranged for on the security of the land, &c., at 4 per cent.

The great demand for Porcelain manufactures which exists in the European and American markets, the excellent site of the Works, and the favourable terms on which it has been bought, the name of the Town, which is known as a household word in connection with the China Manufacture, and the practical knowledge, long experience, and established business connexion which Mr. Phillips is enabled to bring to the Company's affairs, conduce to the belief that the operations of the Company will be commenced with every prospect of success.

Provisional agreements have been entered into as follows :—

An Agreement dated the 22nd day of February, 1877, and made between EDWARD PHILLIPS and WILLIAM LITHERLAND, the vendors, of the one part, and CHARLES KIRK EDDOWES, on behalf of the Company, on the other part.

An Agreement dated the 22nd day of February, 1877, and made between the said E. PHILLIPS of the one part and CHARLES KIRK EDDOWES of the other part.

Acknowledgements

I have had tremendous help from many people in the preparation of this study. I am deeply grateful to them all, and in particular to the following:

Barbara Gregory, my Secretary

Margaret Sargeant, Assistant Curator, Royal Crown Derby Museum

John Twitchett, Curator, Royal Crown Derby Museum

Myra Challand, Royal Crown Derby Guide and Historian

Richard Halliwell, Derby City Museum

Marilyn Swain, Derby Porcelain International Society

Joe Crossley, retired Royal Crown Derby Sliphouse Foreman

Deborah Bates, Royal Doulton Legal Department

Joan Jones, Curator, Minton Museum

Harry Frost, Curator, Dyson Perrins Museum

Henry Sandon, Historian

Geoffrey Godden, Chinaman

Elizabeth Adams, Historian

Richard Kilburn, Historian

The ladies of the Local Studies Library, Derby.

Roy Stott, Managing Director, Gordon Clark Publicity

Peter Bell, descendant of William Litherland

In addition, the following illustrations are included by kind permission of their owners:

pp16 and 25	William Bemrose – Mr. Alan Bemrose
p20	1852 map – The Local Studies Library, Derby
p63	Richard Lunn – Mr. John Twitchett

Hugh Gibson,
Managing Director,
The Royal Crown Derby Porcelain Co. Ltd.,
August, 1992

Index

Abell, Mr, Chairman of Royal
   Worcester,13
Abell, Engine manufacturer of Derby,
   41
Adelphi Hotel, Liverpool, 9, 49, 56
Albert, Prince, 68
Albert Hall, London, 63
American Market, 16, 51, 57, 74
Arboretum, Derby, 11, 22, 44
Arnoux, Leon, Art Director of
   Minton, 46, 47

Backstamps – see Trade Marks
Bakewell, builder, 45, 46
Baldwin, Stanley, 58
Balmoral, 70
Barker, George, engineers, 41, 42, 46
Bemrose, Messrs, printers, 16, 28, 70
Bemrose, Henry Howe, MP, 16, 33
Bemrose, William, 16, 25, 26, 28, 33,
   34, 46, 47, 49, 50, 56, 59, 60, 69
Binns, Richard, 9, 11, 12, 27, 31,
   63, 77
Bradley, Gilbert, 3
Bourne, S and H, modellers, 29
Brookes, builders, 44
Brown, Thomas, raised paste
   gilder, 69
Burne Jones, Lady, 58

Cavendish, Lord Frederick, Chief
   Secretary for Ireland, 66
Cemetery, The Old, Uttoxeter Road,
   Derby, 59
Chaffers, William, author of Marks &
   Monograms, 34
Chapman, J. L., enameller, 69
Charterhouse Street, Royal
   Worcester showrooms, 12, 13, 52
Chetwynd Street, Hadfields mill, 28,
   29, 42
Church Street Works, Hanley, 8

City Art Gallery, Derby, 70
Cockpit Hill, Derby, 28

Derby Crown Porelain Company, 3,
   11, 34, 38, 49, 53, 54, 57, 65, 66, 69,
   71-3, 75-8
Derby Crown Porcelain Factory, 31,
   32,, 37, 38, 41, 47, 65, 67, 69, 74
Devonshire, Duke of, 75
Duesbury Family, 3, 15, 16, 37
Diglis China Works, Worcester, 9, 11

Eddowes, solicitor to Derby Crown
   Porcelain, 29-31, 33-37, 42, 46, 49
Edwardes, J. B., china dealer of
   Folkestone, 48
Evans, Henry, Banker, 33, 34
Everett, Mrs, Edward Phillips'
   housekeeper, 45, 52, 61

Frost, Harry, Curator at Royal
   Worcester, 11, 19
Fryer, George, builder, 56

Goode, Thomas, china dealer, South
   Audley Street, London, 47
Gladstone, W. E., 64-8, 72, 75
Gladstone family, 65-8

Hadfield's Mill, see Chetwynd Street
Hancock, Sampson, 15, 35-7, 74
Harcourt, Sir William, Home
   Secretary, MP for Derby, 65, 66
Hartington, Marquess of, 75
Hawarden Castle, Gladstone's
   country seat, 65, 66, 75
Hextall, solicitor, Derby, 35-7
Hobson, Alderman, 75
Hogg, H. Warrington, modeller, 29
Hough, Tom, company chemist, 41,
   68